THE LEADERSHIP HANDBOOK FOR WOMEN

A Woman's Guide to Developing Leadership Skills for
Career Success, Fostering Equity in Workplace, and
Empowering Other Women to Lead

MONA DAVIS

Contents

Introduction

 "If your actions create a legacy that inspires others to dream more, learn more, do more, and become more, then, you are an excellent leader."

Dolly Parton

Anyone can be a strong leader, but it takes an empowered woman to become a leader that inspires others along the way. With the theme of inequality that exists in nearly every work-place, women are finding it frustrating when they aren't taken seriously in leadership roles. This guide is meant to assist you, no matter what position you are aspiring for. From negotiating your salary to addressing the inequality that you encounter, you are going to learn all of the necessary tips and tricks to become the best leader that you can be. Through your actions, you will also be making the workplace more inclusive for the women who come after you.

In any given field, there are fewer female leaders than male leaders. Because of this gap, there is a noticeable difference in the way that women are treated in the workplace. Only 31% of senior roles are held by women in North America. The percentage is even less in places like Latin America (25%) and the European Union (28%). Since so few women hold these roles, landing them in the first place is a lot harder for women than it is for men. There is a misconception in place that women aren't as experienced or qualified to work in these roles because they hold fewer positions. As you can see, this can become a frustrating loop of biased thinking.

By becoming educated on the issues that women face, you will be able to combat them in your own life. Learning principles that will help you succeed and also earn you respect will allow you to make a name for yourself in any job that you work. You will begin to feel more empowered and better able to stand up for yourself when you are faced with inequality. In doing so, you are also going to serve as a valuable inspiration for those around you. The first step comes from believing in yourself and believing in your ability to work just as hard as anyone else in the office. When you are able to establish your worth, you will be able to convince other people of the same thing.

This topic is important to me because it is also applicable to my own life. I have worked in several jobs where I felt that I was being undervalued solely because I am a woman of color. Instead of speaking up about the issue, I worked in silence while feeling terrible about my situation. I wanted to be a leader, not a follower. I am currently working in STEM and it took me many years to build up my confidence and truly own my role. Once I was finally able to break free of the constructs that were being unfairly placed on me, I realized that my potential was limitless.

I was able to find my place through mentorship. With the help of my mentors who were willing to guide me through my career path, I was able to find inspiration. Now, I believe so much in the power of mentorship and its impacts on minorities in the workplace. Being a female of color, I fell into two of those minorities myself. My mentor showed me how to celebrate my skills and my unique point of view. Instead of being doubtful of my abilities because I was the minority, I was able to see that I had unique ideas to bring to the table. I have a passion for achieving my dreams and I want others to experience the same excitement that I did when I realized that anything is possible if I am willing to put in the work.

ONE

Why Do Companies Refrain from Choosing Women as Leaders?

With all of the inspirational women in the world, you would think that more companies would be open to hiring them for their teams. Instead, women are often met with barriers that are designed to hold them back or teach them that they aren't as worthy of leadership roles as men are. This mindset needs to change in order to empower women to step up and work the roles that they truly qualify to work. There is no reason why a woman can't lead unless she has been taught this by others. Understandably, this can do a lot of damage to your self-confidence, forcing you to believe that you need to work for less pay with less power. In this chapter, you will see why women make such great leaders. You will also be able to gain some inspiration to become a leader yourself.

Women in Leadership Today

Taking a look at the statistics, it is clear to see that women are expected to fill certain roles by those who are considered their superiors. Women hold 44% of all jobs in the United States and

50% of these women work in middle management positions. While this is a great advancement in a management type of role, it is still clear that women are expected to take on less responsibility than men are. In comparison, only 4% of women are Fortune 500 executives. This is a considerable difference when you are looking at things from this perspective.

In the United States, many companies do not show much initiative to get more women in their executive seats. This can prove to be very discouraging when you are a woman looking to land a better job. Comparatively, Norway has actually put a law in place which requires that boards of publicly listed companies must be made up of at least 40% women. Norway is still on its way to reaching this goal, as women still only make up about 38% of all board members. Most countries do not have these laws in place, which means that women need to fend for themselves in the workplace, hoping to prove that they belong in these top leadership positions.

Another interesting view of women in leadership comes from taking a closer look at how female bosses are treated. Normally, a boss is respected to the highest degree. Certain studies have shown that female bosses actually still face gender discrimination and are not being taken as seriously as male bosses. In general, it appears that employees are less likely to take criticism from a woman and that is due to the societal expectations that were put in place long ago. Women were meant to be subservient, only answering to men. Times have changed since then, but unfortunately, some people still have these outdated perceptions when it comes to the way that women should be treated.

Other studies have shown that people often expect female bosses to be more caring and understanding. Therefore, they expect a female boss to give them praise where they would expect a male boss to give them criticism. When people are shown the opposite of what they expect, no matter what that is, this usually leads to a negative reaction. This is part of the reason why female bosses aren't seen as powerful or wise. They are normally placed into a caregiver role, even when it comes to the professional workplace. When employees are unable to see a female boss as being on the same level as a male boss, they are going to treat them differently.

In order to make sure that changes are being implemented, companies must see the feedback that they are getting as valuable. Getting feedback from employees as well as management can showcase what some of the issues are within the company. If people are able to express their opinions in private, they are more likely to be honest. Sometimes, when given this opportunity, people openly admit to their biases. When this is known, the company can do more to promote an atmosphere of inclusivity, showing their workers that discriminatory behavior is unacceptable.

Myths About Women Leaders

It is often said that more women in management means more competitive attitudes. While this would be considered healthy if it were men competing for a title, women are often expected to have a "queen bee" attitude, meaning that they want to get ahead even if it means putting their competition down. While this isn't always true, men often believe that too many powerful women in one place can only result in a catfight. You can see why this is a ridiculous conclusion to jump to, suggesting that women can't support other women. This is why being an inspirational leader is going to prove all of these people wrong. It will help them see that they are thinking about things in a closed-minded approach.

Another myth that is in place is that some people do not believe that women have the necessary skills in order to be placed in leadership positions. This skewed perception still exists, even as women train alongside men in prestigious universities while earning the same degrees. People still make it a point to say that women are bad at negotiating or that they won't have the drive necessary to get ahead at work because they are too focused on their marriages and children. Men who have families and even men who are shy do not get placed into these boxes nearly as much as women do. As a woman, these things will get used against you frequently in the workplace.

The bottom line is that women are as capable as they want to be. Aside from their gender, there is nothing that differentiates them from their male peers. A lot of people also believe that women want to work in these roles and fill these positions just to prove a point. They are not seen as individuals with goals and dreams. While women are proving a point when they are able to successfully work these positions, they are likely doing so for a reason that goes way beyond proving to men that they can. Women should not have to prove anything in order to be treated with the same respect.

Any woman who works hard for their leadership role is likely going to perform just as well as anyone else would. In fact, because there are so many odds against women in the work-place, you are likely to find that women will be willing to work harder and put more effort into their roles. With all of these myths surrounding women in leadership, it is no wonder that so many females are discouraged on a daily basis. You have likely felt this way if you have ever wanted to move up to a higher position at your current job. While you might feel that you have all of the qualifications and experience necessary, you will also likely feel that a man with the same skills would be more likely to earn the job over you.

It is unfortunate that these myths exist, but it is necessary to acknowledge them in order to show people that they are only myths. Prove others wrong by being the exact opposite of what they expect you to be. Understand that the only way to fight for equality is by working hard and showing people exactly what you have to offer. Protesting these myths is likely only going to lead to more discrimination or a label that suggests you are difficult to work with. Prove them wrong by showing them what you are capable of. Allow them to see your skills without you having to provide an explanation.

Barriers Faced and Solutions to Those Barriers

There are four main types of barriers that women will face in leadership. These barriers are seen time and time again, often wearing women down and leading them to believe that they do not have what it takes to make a great leader. If you have ever experienced any of these things for yourself, know that you are not alone. So many other women have also experienced these barriers, but there are always going to be solutions for them. The following are the main barriers that you will likely encounter as you work toward your leadership position:

- Structural: A structural barrier exists when women are left out from normal workplace interactions. For example, when everyone finishes a big project and goes out for drinks, a woman might not be invited because others assume that she has to get home to her family. Another example is when employees decide to meet on the golf course on the weekends, yet they do not think to invite a female employee because they automatically assume she will not be interested in golf. This barrier exists simply due to the fact that people make assumptions. Everyone can benefit from making fewer assumptions. If you ever feel that your peers are making these assumptions, speak up for yourself. Tell them that you would like to go out for drinks too or that you actually really enjoy golfing. This will allow them to see that you aren't afraid to earn your place.

- Institutional: The role of the leader has been deemed a masculine role for the last several decades. Even with the rise in the fight for female equality, many people still see the role as one that belongs to a man. When given the choice, many people would simply pick a man for the role because they feel that men are more powerful and stronger. This stereotyping is something that has been in place for a long time, but that doesn't mean that it cannot be changed. Use your voice to stand up for women's rights. There are no such things as male traits and female traits.

- Individual: This barrier comes from within. It is the self-doubt that you hold onto, even when you know that you are qualified to be a leader. This doubt tends to come in when you begin second-guessing your choices. It can be hard to be the only one who is fighting for your leadership position, but sometimes, that is the way that things are. Build yourself up with plenty of self-confidence and motivation by reading about other inspirational women. Think about those in your life who inspire you, too.

- Lifestyle: Having a great work/family balance can be hard, but it is not impossible. There are many men in leadership roles who have families, just as women do. Because women are seen as caregivers though, they are also seen as leaders who would not be willing to devote as much time to their work as men would. This is simply untrue because this trait is completely individual. Gender does not matter when it comes to the way that you decide you want to devote yourself to your work. It can be frustrating to be put into a box where people assume that you are not willing to do certain things simply because you have a family or because you are a mother.

If you have yet to experience any of these barriers, you are likely to encounter them over time. Sometimes, these barriers can be annoying. Other times, they can be truly debilitating and discouraging. Understand that you do not have to succumb to these roles that others are trying to place you in. Knowing where you stand and being able to stand your ground is important. It will allow you to keep pushing forward, even when others would expect you to give up. Prove to all those people, and yourself, that you have exactly what it takes to be a great leader.

As mentioned, having a mentor is going to serve you well. This is a person who has likely gone through all of the above barriers before. When you are able to hear about real-life experiences and how they were handled, you should feel a lot more inspired to tackle your own barriers. Changing institutional barriers has proven to be a lot harder because this is a mindset that has been ingrained into our heads for such a long time. Instead of trying to change the entire mindset, change the minds of those around you. Show your peers exactly why you are a great leader and why that mindset does not apply to you or your skills.

The final step comes when you can ensure that you are mentally strong enough to balance your own personal life and your work life. This can be a challenge for many reasons, but you need to make sure that you are on your own team. If you are constantly putting yourself down with negative self-talk, you can expect your results to turn out the same way. Praise yourself and recognize all that you have accomplished so far. Set goals for yourself that are challenging enough to motivate you. Allow yourself enough time to excel at work as well as excel at being a great wife and mother. The balance is not impossible, as long as you are willing to work hard.

Why Women Make Great Leaders

- They Are Empathetic: Generally speaking, women value relationships and have the tendency to understand others. This is important no matter what business you are involved in. Having the necessary interpersonal relationship skills is what will allow you to succeed. Being great at your job is much more than doing the work that you are given. It extends to the connections that you make and the way that you are able to communicate with your peers. Having empathy is helpful because it will allow you to be more open-minded about the way that you approach situations.
- They Are Great Listeners: Being able to communicate effectively in business is a must, but communication goes beyond speaking. The other half of communication stems from how well you can listen. Being an active listener is going to prove to others that you care about what is being said and women are great at this. Women tend to cling to each detail of what is being said, analyzing the information as a whole. When no detail is spared, the other person should truly feel that they are being heard.
- They Focus on Teamwork: Women are typically filled with passion and enthusiasm. While they are able to lead in certain situations, they are also able to work with others as a team. Because of their drive and their ability to get ahead as a group rather than an individual,

success is going to come naturally. So many leaders can be great at what they do, but they are lacking in teamwork skills. Being great as a group tends to drive women to do even better.

- They Are Good at Multitasking: Being able to juggle tasks is often necessary when you are working a job that requires you to have a lot of responsibility. Women are able to do this because this is how their brains are wired. On any given day, women must be able to divide their attention between their spouse, their children, themselves, and their job. This is why they are typically so great at multitasking; it comes naturally.

- They Excel at Communication: Because women are often put down or second-guessed while at work, they tend to be great at communicating their thoughts and ideas. When someone has to work twice as hard to express themselves, this allows for a lot of practice with the verbalization of their feelings. Women also typically enjoy communicating a lot more than men do. They are willing to discuss topics that they might not agree with, yet they are able to work through them in an eloquent manner.

- They Handle Crisis Situations Well: At work, there are going to be times of uncertainty where everything feels like it is going to fall apart. Women are experts at holding things together. While often being placed in this role in their personal lives, women know how to remain calm under this kind of pressure and stress. They are fixers and they will look at every option that they can when it comes to avoiding a crisis. This is a very valuable trait to hold, especially for those jobs that are fast-paced and unpredictable.

- They Have High Emotional Intelligence: Being intelligent is a desirable skill, but having emotional intelligence is arguably even more desirable. When you are able to understand others on an emotional level, you are going to know how to talk to them and how to work with them. Women have a great perception of the emotional intelligence of others. They are also usually very in-tune with their own. Because of this, they will find it easy to relate to others and to approach things in a very personable manner.

- They Defy Odds: As you have seen, the statistics clearly showcase that women are underrepresented in just about every workplace that you can think of. Because of this, they are constantly defying their own odds as they earn leadership positions. This places a lot of pressure on women to live up to the expectations that are being placed on them. Women do this effortlessly, proving each day why they deserve to be there by working hard to stay on top.

- They Can Wear Many Hats: When placed in a leadership position, it is often required that you must go with the flow. Women are experts at this because this is how they tend to live their lives already. From being a wife to being a mother, women are already expected to fill many roles on a daily basis. Even in friendship, women can be exactly what their friends need them to be. It only makes sense that they would apply the same principles in the workplace. They find it easy to juggle these roles, thriving while doing so.

TWO

What Type of Leader Are You?

In order to become a successful leader, you do not need to place yourself in a box. There are many different leadership styles that are equally valid and respected. Knowing what kind of leader you are will help you better understand yourself and the way that you interact with your peers. Because each workplace is different, there are certain leadership styles that will work better at specified places. Having this knowledge about leadership can help you to become the best possible leader you can be. Even if you think you have all of the skills necessary in order to succeed, there is always going to be room for improvement.

Types of Leaders

Do you know what kind of leader you are? The way that you take on your role is very important to your success. These are some of the most common leadership styles that are found in various workplaces. Chances are, you will be able to identify with one or more of these leadership styles. In an attempt to better your skills, pay attention to the different strengths that each one of these styles encompasses.

Autocratic

This is a strong, yet one-dimensional, leadership style. It is a straightforward approach in which the leader believes that they should have all of the decision-making power. Anyone who is below them must report to them. Often, this type of leader will not feel the need to consult with their subordinates in order to make decisions. It is only after the decisions are made that an autocratic leader will feel as though the rest of the team should be notified. There is a lot of confidence present behind each action that is taken. If any instructions are given to others, this type of leader will expect them to be handled immediately. There is definitely a sense of pride present when it comes to this leadership style.

This type of leader would likely clash with their peers in most modern-day workplaces. People tend to favor leaders who are willing to hear input from their peers. This can cause conflicts because those who are not in charge might feel as though their opinions don't matter. It is easy to become consumed by power if you are not careful with this leadership style.

Democratic

A very common approach, having a democratic leadership style is usually favorable for most people. Because others enjoy being heard, they will feel that their opinions are valued when they are being guided by a democratic leader. This type of leader will always encourage participation and be eager to hear about the opinions of others. Communication is always present, ensuring that everyone has their own voice. People can be individuals without being seen in a negative light, even if their opinions differ from those of the leader. Without a doubt, a democratic approach is what is most preferred by every workplace.

This type of leadership works very well if you want to keep your team organized. When everyone feels that they have a purpose, they are going to be more likely to stay on top of their responsibilities. This type of leadership highlights that each step taken is an important one. That means that each decision made by each person matters toward the overall bigger picture. It is typically a pleasant experience to work with a democratic leader because you will be able to voice your own opinions, even if you are not in charge.

Coaching

Taking a mentor approach, a leader who coaches doesn't lead directly. Instead, they will push others to think for themselves and to come up with their own solutions. In turn, that person is being guided toward learning instead of simply taking instructions. Naturally, this leadership style is less structured. It still remains a very effective form of leadership to this day. Instead of feeling like you are being bossed around, a coaching leader takes on the role of a teacher rather than a boss. This can prove to boost employee confidence levels, as well as increase their skills.

With this type of leadership, everyone in the workplace learns together at the same rate. It can become a very solid form of team-building, no matter what you are doing. By keeping everyone motivated at all times, this leader tends to bring forth a positive approach on a daily basis. Because of this optimism, those who are under this kind of leadership tend to be in happier moods and are able to work through difficult problems when they are encountered. Having a coach as a leader also provides flexibility for those who have difficulty with authority figures.

Strategic

This kind of leader is very influential to their peers. Instead of directing them toward certain decisions or actions, a strategic leader carefully selects their own behaviors in order to allow others to follow suit. While their peers will come to these conclusions on their own, it is through the direct influence of the strategic leader. In order to do this, there is a lot of leading by example. This means that a strategic leader must be very careful with the way that they present themselves and their own behaviors. They must be a model employee so that others can learn to be like them.

Under this kind of leadership, you can expect a team that is on the same page. Each member of the team will be well-trained and readily equipped with the skills that they need in order to succeed on their own. This type of leadership is contagious because it teaches employees the exact principles necessary to lead on their own in the future. While being able to handle unforeseen risks and other threats, those guided by a strategic leader will see problem-solving as a welcomed task.

Transformational

This is a very progressive form of leadership. A transformational leader is always seeking out ways to make the workplace better. From adopting new habits to finding different ways to teach their peers, a transformational leader has the desire to have a work environment that is thriving. This kind of leader is likely to set a lot of goals with deadlines that are challenging. By pushing others outside of their comfort zones, a transformational leader would hope that this brings forth excellence. This kind of leader is guaranteed to provide you with many challenges that you must face as a learning tool.

Some people might find it difficult to work with such a leader because the demand can be high at times. If you are able to understand that this is all going to benefit the bigger picture, it might be easier to accept this leadership style. This kind of leader will encourage you to complete goals while also having your own personal goals to work toward. At no point in time should you feel that you are simply doing busywork to pass the time. Each moment is seen as valuable.

Laissez-faire

This is a French word that translates to "let them do." Gathering from this definition, the Laissez-faire leadership style is more relaxed than some of the others that have been discussed. Its principles focus on allowing people to learn at their own pace. While the leader will delegate certain responsibilities, it is then up to the individual to work through them with their own method of choice. There will be minimal interference from the leader as the individual works.

To some, this leadership style works very well because of all the flexibility involved. As long as the employees are motivated on their own, this can be a very successful method to utilize. It only becomes a problem for those who are not self-disciplined. When you are not constantly being supervised, this gives you more room to learn and grow. Every decision that is made is on you, providing you with a sense of greater responsibility. Because you are being encouraged to think for yourself and on your own time, this will allow you to prepare yourself for the future when you will potentially end up in a leadership position.

Charismatic

This leadership style revolves around the person's natural ability to be charming and motivated toward others. They are typically very passionate and confident leaders who have no trouble showing their peers exactly what must be done. These leaders will not feel that they have to prove anything to those that work under them. Instead, they will aim to share their wisdom with the rest of the team, encouraging each person to bring out their own natural sense of charisma.

People often see this type of leadership as less successful because it can appear to take a self-centered approach. If the leader is charismatic, yet they do not know how to use their skills to help others, they can come across as selfish. Nobody enjoys working under someone who only seems to care about themselves. This kind of leadership is all about balance and stability. If the leader is not a stable person, then the entire team will not be stable. When taking on this type of leadership style, you must be very careful that you do not let the power get to your head. By remaining humble, you should still be able to help your team learn something and become more valuable along the way.

Understanding Your Leadership Style

We all have our own strengths and weaknesses, regardless of how we lead. By getting to know these strengths and weaknesses, you are going to have an advantage by knowing how you need to improve your skills. By taking a proactive approach, you are going to be able to lead your team effortlessly while also identifying ways that you can become a better leader. It is all a big process of trial and error, one that requires patience to understand. Most people see their weaknesses as downfalls, but instead, you can think of them as areas that need more work. Consider your strengths and see if there are any ways that you can use them to boost some of your weaknesses.

When you have a particular leadership style, you should own it. This is an aspect of your personality. While you can always improve on your leadership skills, being confident in the one that you have will show others that you want to be taken seriously. If you waiver in your faith, others are not going to trust you either. You've likely heard of the saying, "fake it till you make it," and this is a good way to approach your leadership style. This does not mean that you shouldn't improve and become a better leader, but you need to have confidence in your abilities before you can convince others that they should listen to you.

There are factors to consider when determining if your leadership style is the best for the given job that you have. The environment in which you work will shape the way that you must lead. Is your company strict or relaxed? Depending on how much freedom the employees have on a typical day, this is going to determine how much guidance they will need. If you provide too much or too little, this is going to offset the balance. Study the work environment and then make your best decision on what your peers are going to need from you.

Your communication style is essential to your leadership style. You must be aware of how your peers are responding to your requests and guidance. If you feel that you aren't getting through to them, you might need to take a different approach. A healthy leadership style will come with clear communication that is tailored to the given group of people that you are meant to lead. There should not be any confusion or misunderstanding when you instruct your peers. If they have any questions, they should feel comfortable enough to ask you in order to gain clarity. Employees who feel like they cannot talk to their leaders have a higher likelihood of being unhappy at work. You should aim to make your peers feel as comfortable as possible while still maintaining the structure that they need.

Each workplace is going to come with its unique set of challenges. These are often unpredictable and stressful, but a good leader must be able to adapt at any time. Being set in your ways can be a good thing, but you also need to have a sense of flexibility in order to make sure that you have enough back-up plans to protect you. Different leaders are going to come up with different ways to solve problems. Your problem-solving skills are essential because they not only serve in your best interest but in the best interest of the rest of the team too. By working together as a whole, you should all be able to move forward in success. When only the leader is successful, the rest of the team suffers.

Your leadership style is likely inspired by other leaders that you have had in your own life. Through learning from them, you have likely formed opinions about which methods work and which ones do not. You know how you like to be taught, so it makes sense that you would model your approach after your own experiences. This is a good foundation for your leadership style, but do not forget that you need to look at your team as a group of individuals. Certain people might need extra guidance from you or additional resources. Part of being a great leader comes from being able to pay attention to your team and determine what they need from you.

When you keep the lines of communication open, your team is going to feel comfortable about coming to you when they are in need of more help or guidance. Try your best to always be there for them, as your past leaders and mentors were there for you. When you keep paying it forward, this is going to create more great leaders in the future. As a female, you can likely identify with how important it is to make a good name for yourself in the workplace. Since you are being judged harder than men who hold the same position, you often need to work twice as hard to prove the same point.

Leadership Styles per Gender

There are many differences between the ways that men and women lead in the workplace. While there are instances in which all of the above leadership styles would be effective, there does tend to be a pattern between the roles that men choose versus the roles women choose. Generally speaking, women tend to take a coaching approach that is filled with plenty of guidance and communication. Because women tend to enjoy nurturing, they are fulfilled when they can see that the team is succeeding as a whole. Women know that their actions are directly responsible for whether the team is going to work well together. They hold this responsibility very close to them, often willing to take the blame for mistakes that are made.

Men tend to take on a more direct approach. They like to state their commands or instructions and then wait for their team to comply. While this method is not any better or worse than that of the coaching method, it is different. This leadership style works well for people who are self-motivated or comfortable with figuring problems out on their own, but it can often make those who are more timid feel inadequate. When there is little to no guidance, the team is more likely to make mistakes or to feel that they cannot complete their tasks. Men often see things as very black or white, believing if they can see what needs to be done, everyone else will be able to see it too.

Women tend to view the workplace as a transformational space. They are not afraid to think outside of the box and use creativity to make improvements. When it comes to developing new skills, women love to inspire others through leading by example. This transformation is usually seen as a goal in the way that women lead. For men, there is more of a sense of tradition behind the way that they lead. For centuries now, a hierarchical approach has been taken. Men tend to see this as a sign that they should not fix something that isn't broken. Because they were effortlessly woven into the leadership role throughout history, men are less likely to take a transformative approach. They will more likely aim to keep the structure traditional.

Interestingly enough, studies have shown that female leaders are more effective in female-dominated settings while male leaders are more effective in male-dominated settings. These results speak to the fact that each gender is most comfortable leading those who they feel they can identify with. It becomes a different kind of leadership experience when you must lead a group that is very different from you. Not being able to see eye-to-eye is one of the most common reasons why a team does not respect a leader. For this reason, a good leader should always be adaptable and understanding. Women do have an advantage here because they are usually more willing to change, whereas men are more likely to refuse change and attempt to use the same methods that they already know.

None of the leadership styles discussed are innately more "masculine" or "feminine." There are definitely female leaders that decide to take on a more hardened approach, while there are also male leaders that choose an interpersonal style. The great thing about leadership is that it evolves with you as a person. If you want to be the most effective female leader that you can be, you must first understand the expectations that others have of you. While comparing these expectations to the skills that you have to offer, know that you are a valuable asset to any team. Understand that you can be a great leader and you can also adapt when you must.

THREE

Bringing Yourself to the Table (If You Want To)

Not every woman desires a seat in power, but there are quite a few that are aiming for one. Having this goal is not ridiculous or beyond your grasp. Just because there are more men in these roles than women does not mean that you should keep yourself out of the running. Instead, you must do the opposite. Continue to push forward, even when others doubt you. Allow yourself to shine by using your strengths to get you further. If you have high hopes of taking on a big role, then this chapter is for you. While learning how to harness your skills in order to allow them to work for you, these tips are going to help you land the position of your dreams.

Do You Have What It Takes?

It is no secret that self-confidence will get you far in life. If you do not believe in yourself, then you likely cannot fathom how other people are supposed to believe in you. Addressing any insecurities before you start working on big goals is important. You need to come from a place of confidence and bravery. Even when the odds look less than optimistic, what matters most is how you carry yourself. Celebrate each turning point with the promise that you will continue to do even better; learn from each mistake and understand that you are not invincible. Big leaders must have a sense of humility in order to truly succeed. Nothing good ever comes from bullying others or putting others down so you can get ahead.

It takes a thick skin to hold a position of power. You are going to be subject to plenty of criticism, some constructive and some not. If you find that you are easily broken down by the opinions of others, this is definitely something that you will need to work on before you secure your leadership role. Everyone is going to have something to say about what you are doing but as long as you know that you are working hard and being fair, you should not allow these opinions to sway your judgment. A lot of people give in to the pressure that comes from this criticism. It can be a lot to handle, but if you prepare for it and know that you live by your own principles, then you should be just fine.

As mentioned, being a great leader all comes down to having an understanding of your own strengths and weaknesses. Once these have been identified, you are going to know what you excel in and what you need to improve on. You will also be able to better transform your weaknesses, choosing to turn them into strengths instead of viewing them as a downfall to your personality. There are many different ways that you can begin embracing your strengths and you can start immediately. The sooner you decide to take action, the sooner you are going to land the leadership role that you have been working so hard to obtain.

Write down all of your strengths. Being able to see a tangible list of your strengths will serve as a reminder of what you are good at already. You should not try to change these things about yourself. Simply write them down and acknowledge them. Next, write down what you would consider your weaknesses. After you have written them all down, do your best to not immediately jump into the mindset of having to change yourself. Instead, compare your strengths and weaknesses. Are there any ways that you can connect the two in order to improve on the areas that need improvement?

A common mistake that is made is that you think you will need to let go of or change all of your weaknesses. Not only is this unrealistic, but it is unnecessary. You should not have to change who you are as a person in order to utilize the leadership skills that you naturally possess. Think of yourself as a project that you are working on at all times, and there is always room for improvement. Because you have been working on this for a lifetime, it wouldn't make sense to start from the very beginning. By acknowledging the foundation that you already have, you can build on it. Seek inspiration from others, learn new skills, and do everything that you can to prove to yourself that you are a true leader.

Half of proving yourself as a leader comes from convincing yourself that you belong there. When your mind is working against you, that negativity is going to impact the way that you work. Instead of motivating yourself to keep going until you reach the top, you are going to be met with doubts and negative self-talk. When you know how to combat these things that your own mind creates, you will be a lot more likely to let them roll off your shoulders if you are treated this way by others. Most of us would agree that we are our own worst critics. We know ourselves best, so we often feel that we have to be extra critical. Try your best to only treat yourself with the same respect that you hope others will give you.

How to Earn Your Seat at the Table

Setting goals is the very first step. When you realize that you want something, turn that into a goal. Use the motivation that you feel to fuel you each day. It is important that you are very clear with yourself about what you want and when you hope to accomplish it. If you set loose goals for yourself, then it will be sending the message that your successes won't matter as much. By putting a little bit of necessary pressure on yourself, you will learn how to value your own hard work. Understand that each setback you encounter is just going to serve as a small road-block along the way. You will have to trust in yourself to be able to go around these things and keep sight of your goals.

Being organized and motivated are two essential skills that a lot of companies look for in a leader. If you cannot keep track of your own goals and progress, then it is unlikely that you are going to be able to do so for an entire team. Keeping this in mind, know that you need to track your progress. If you realize that your goals aren't being met, make changes. Do whatever you can in order to secure your success. Once you are able to see your end result, you are going to feel great and ready to take on even more goals. To boost your skills, get a mentor, read plenty of books on leadership, and do everything you can to learn about your given industry. Knowledge is power.

The following are some simple tips that you can use to improve your work performance and ensure that you are prepared to take on a larger role:

- Handle Tasks by Priority: Any given person is going to have a to-do list that is filled with tasks of importance, but do you know which of your tasks are the *most* important? Working by priority is the key to successfully securing nearly any leadership position.

When you work this way, you will never miss important deadlines. Being able to set aside certain tasks for later so that you can focus on the more pressing ones is important to learn how to do. While you might be a go-getter, wanting to finish everything at once, this isn't going to benefit your productivity. You only get so many hours in a day, so you need to use them wisely.

- Practice Your Communication: Before you speak, you need to think about all of the different factors involved. Those who are quick to express an opinion before thinking it over can often find themselves in conflicts or altercations. Not only should you think before you speak, but you should also listen attentively. When you are able to hear other perspectives, you will better understand the role that you play. Know that you might change your mind and that is okay. By keeping an open mind, you are going to be an easier person to talk to.

- Don't Put Off Difficult Tasks: Getting into the habit of putting something off because it is difficult can push you into procrastination. Just because something is challenging you does not mean that it will get any easier if you put it off. Taking a short break can give your brain the necessary rejuvenation that it needs, but when you completely walk away from a task, you are admitting defeat. Make sure that you are honoring yourself by believing in your skills. Tackle the hard tasks right away and you won't have to deal with them later on.

- Eliminate Distractions: Distractions can come in all shapes and sizes. From your phone screen to your friends who want to go out every night, you need to make smart decisions regarding the things that are keeping you from reaching your goals. We all need time to unwind and have fun, but this should only happen while you are not working. If you split your focus between work and fun, both things are going to be compromised. Instead, finish each task entirely before you move onto the next one. Getting into this habit will keep your brain more focused on what you are doing at the moment and less likely to wander.

How to Get Noticed

You will receive an invitation to the table when you can do two things — prove you are worthy of being there and show your initiative and commitment to the cause. There are five ways that are proven to be very effective for getting noticed by people who can give you a higher leadership position. When you can become proficient at these things, you will have much more self-confidence and a true purpose for why you are there. Giving yourself this kind of structure is going to help you stay on track and allow you to see that anything is possible, as long as you keep reaching for your goals.

1. Ask to Be Included in Executive Leadership Meetings: When you are given the chance to be a part of these meetings, take an active role by making sure that you take plenty of notes and ask questions of importance. When you can show that you have initiative before you are officially given a big leadership role, you will be bound to impress those who are in charge of making the decision. You will also be able to see a larger picture of the company, realizing that every decision made by these top executives is going to impact those who work underneath them. As you listen to these strategies, see if you can determine how you'd make the workplace better for all.

2. Demonstrate a Sense of Curiosity: Being curious shows that you have been thinking about a topic, even when you weren't required to. Approaching any task or problem with a sense of curiosity will allow you to think creatively in order to sort it out. When you can not only determine why something happened but also when and how, you are likely going to be able to think of plenty of additional solutions for solving these issues. If you have time to spare when you are off-hours, it wouldn't hurt to put some research into your company or the role that you want. Being willing to think about both of these things on your own time shows that you truly value the job.

3. Act as an Expert: When you are talking to any high-level executive at your company, imagine yourself as being on the same level. Do not sink down into a subservient role. Know that you have your own set of skills and valuable knowledge that would make a generous contribution to the overall success of the company. Acknowledge that you have been working very hard to get where you are so far and that your journey doesn't end here. You can always take it farther if you are willing to put in the effort and look the part. In doing so, this will also boost your self-confidence levels.

4. Build Important Work-Related Relationships: Talking to people is a very important skill that all high-level executives need to master. You will need to be able to not only talk to your peers but your clients. The way that you communicate and present yourself will often be a make it or break it moment in the way that you do business. When you are a likable and approachable person, you will find that it is a lot easier to cultivate these relationships. Being closed off and guarded is only going to make communication more difficult for you.

You need to be able to talk to all kinds of people and treat them with the same level of respect, no matter what they can do for you.

5. Always Prioritize: The way you approach the job is something that must also be prioritized. If you keep trying the same strategies over and over again, only to be met with the same results, you need to take this as a sign to try something new. Prioritize your success over your unwillingness to change the routines that you already know. By breaking outside of these comfort zones, you are going to be able to have new experiences. Your desire for success on an executive level will be obtained and you will allow yourself to keep learning new skills along the way. Even for an executive, the learning never ends.

Negotiate Your Worth

Getting the job is only part of the battle that is won. As a woman, you must also be aware that you need to stand up for your worth. Because of the gender income gap, women earn less to the dollar when compared to the amount that men are able to earn. By default, employers tend to offer women lower salaries, even when they are working the same jobs as male executives. Having an awareness of this should boost your desire to get paid as much as you believe you are worth. In order to do so, you must be willing to negotiate. By giving yourself a voice, you are showing your bosses that you know you are valuable.

Before you meet with your bosses to confirm that you would like the position being offered, do some research. When you know what the average salary is for the job, then you will be able to confirm if you are being impacted by the gender wage gap or not. It is suggested that you think of four different compensation packages that you would be okay with taking. Even if this is your dream job, you should never settle for less than you deserve. Otherwise, you will be taking on the same amount of work for only a portion of the salary you had hoped for.

Never undersell yourself. If you get into the meeting and your weaknesses are brought up, don't let the conversation stay there for long. Instead of agreeing with these points, bring up strengths that you know you have. By showing them what you have to offer instead of simply agreeing with your downfalls, this is going to highlight what you plan on bringing to the table. Talk about milestones that you have accomplished and the goals that you have reached. Let them know what you plan on accomplishing in the future, too.

Do your best to not simply adopt male characteristics. This tends to happen when women get opportunities that are hard to come by. The pressures of being in a male-dominated industry can often get into your head. You do not need to change who you are in order to successfully negotiate your terms to your employer. They should be willing to accept you for you are and what you are able to offer the company. It is never a good idea to force anything about your persona because being ingenuine is going to get old. When you can be yourself from the beginning, you are going to be a lot happier when you get the job.

During your meeting, do not apologize for negotiating your compensation. You deserve to earn enough money to live happily and comfortably. Consider if a male candidate were in your position. Do you think they would feel the need to apologize at any point during their interview? By getting rid of these gender roles that have developed over time in the workplace, you have the chance to completely change the narrative. Know that you are grateful for the opportunity, yet also make sure that you are recognizing how valuable you are.

Before you take on the opportunity, make sure that you know how to own your confidence. If you start a job with insecurities, they are only going to worsen over time. Know that you deserve to be there just as much as any man or woman. Without shrinking down in order to make yourself more acceptable, you will be able to see that your strengths should be celebrated. If you do not believe this yourself, it is going to be hard to convince others to see this, especially those who are in high positions of power. By showing your bosses that you can be comfortable at a high level of leadership, they are going to have confidence in you from the very beginning.

Whether you have to recite positive affirmations in the mirror each morning before you go to work or if you have to give yourself weekly pep talks, find ways that you can boost your self-confidence before you have your big interview. When you can enter the room feeling great about the skills you have to offer, you are going to have a higher likelihood of landing the job. Those who are insecure about their skills still have some work to do before they can be placed in high leadership roles. A leader should be fearless and confident. Even if you aren't, you should know how to make people think that you are.

FOUR

Overcoming Your Fear

W hile climbing the corporate ladders, facing your fears is bound to happen. There will be many new challenges and obstacles that you will encounter when you seek a higher leadership position. Fear isn't a bad thing; it keeps you grounded and ready to learn. Fear can even be a great motivational tool if you know how to use it correctly. Whether the fear comes from within or is triggered by the expectations of those around you, know that perfection does not exist. You are going to be afraid sometimes, but this isn't going to stop you. Instead, you are going to learn how to turn all of your fears into productive ways to keep pushing forward and reaching your goals.

This chapter is going to provide you with several real strategies that you can use to conquer your own fears. The key to this is all about changing your mindset. If you go to work thinking that you cannot be as great of a leader as a man can be, then you are right. Don't doubt yourself from the very beginning! Instead, prove to everyone and yourself that you have what it takes. These strategies are among the most common because they show high success rates. Like any habit, being fearful and living with a negative mindset is going to be a process to change. It isn't impossible, though!

Common Fears

1. Being an Imposter: This fear is based on the way that you feel about yourself. As you work in your office, you might be plagued with feelings that you don't belong there or that you are not worthy of being a part of the team. This can make you feel like an imposter. Imposter syndrome is very common, especially for those who have recently earned positions in power. Know that you deserve to be there just as much as the next person does. Make it a point to prove this to yourself each day.

2. Being Criticized: It can be hard to hear criticism, but leaders often must be subject to it in order to know that they are doing their jobs properly. Try not to take criticism too personally. Know that it is supposed to be constructive and you should be using it to make you a better leader. It does not reflect on your ability to successfully work the job that you have or live the life that you live. When you can separate your emotions from the criticism, you will be better able to take it into consideration.

3. Being a Failure: This is one of the most common fears experienced by those who work a high-ranking job. Failure is a devastating thought, especially when so many others are counting on you. This can place a lot of pressure on your shoulders, threatening to push you to a breaking point. What you need to remember is that you must stay calm. As soon as you give in to this pressure and fear, then your work will be compromised.

Know that taking a few deep breaths and regrouping can come in handy.

4. Being Bad at Communication: With the way that good communication is stressed, having a fear that you are bad at communication makes sense. It isn't easy for everyone to talk to people. This can simply be due to a personality type, but it is still important that you do your best to practice your skills. As you know, being able to communicate is very important, no matter what aspect of business you are dealing with. If you cannot convey your message, then you won't be able to do your job. Understand that we are all human beings. You will have bad days and you will have good days. Know that others are also no exception.

5. Making Hard Decisions: You can guarantee that, as a leader, you will be faced with some hard decision-making tasks. This is what leaders are for. They must make the hard choices on behalf of the team. Your critical thinking skills are going to come in handy here. You need to be able to use them carefully while making a decision without too much deliberation. As you become more experienced in leadership, you will realize that there is a right balance between debating your choices and finally making your selection.

6. Not Taking Responsibility: As your responsibilities begin to pile on, you might have a fear that you will simply delegate all of the tasks to other people. This can feel as though you are just rerouting all responsibility away from yourself. Being a leader does involve some delegation, but at the end of the day, your team's success falls on you. If a mistake is made, this becomes your fault. You need to be accepting of the fact that you hold the responsibility by default, so it makes sense that you would put in the work in order to maintain it.

7. Not Getting it Done: This is a fairly simple fear that most can relate with — not reaching goals can be a scary thought. When you are working on your own goals, the pressure is lessened. However, when you are in leadership, your goals are going to affect a lot more people. Try not to become distracted. While distractions help calm you down, they simply delay your work even further. When you can stay focused on what really matters, you will be proving to yourself that you can and will get it done.

No matter what fears you face, you must be able to identify them. This is going to make you an even stronger leader because it follows the principle that nobody is perfect. Even if you were to look closely at your own boss or mentor, you would find that they are sometimes ruled by fears of their own. The way that you are able to identify these fears and live with them will say a lot about your character. Fears do not have to debilitate you or stop you. Instead, you can make them work for you, just like your weaknesses. Train yourself to see your fears without backing down. Just because you reach them does not mean that you must stop; keep going. Push past them and prove that you can continue doing your best.

Train yourself to see your fears as challenges to overcome instead of roadblocks. While they might delay your progress temporarily, know that this isn't going to stop you from being a great leader. You will learn the most effective strategies to get past your fears and work toward goals that you know you can accomplish. When you have all of the steps that you need, the only thing you will need to do is enforce them. Everyone has fears, even the most fearless leaders. They didn't reach this point by giving up and that is what you have to remember about yourself, as well.

How to Overcome Your Fears

Getting over your fears can be easier said than done. Taking the real-life example of Alexandria Ocasio-Cortez, you will realize that she didn't become a powerful leader overnight. She first had to overcome her fear of speaking up in Congress, a huge part of her job that led her to the success that she has today. Ocasio-Cortez has stated that she began using her fear as a "guiding light" rather than a stopping point. By switching over to this mentality, she was able to clearly see which of the skills she needed to work on. One of the worst things that can happen to you, even worse than failure, is becoming stagnant. When you give up of your own accord, this is solely the fear ruling over you.

Ocasio-Cortez became the youngest person in US history to be elected to congress. Because of her age and her position as a young female in leadership, this has led to a lot of backlash from her peers and critics alike. However, Ocasio-Cortez continues to persist despite what others have to say about her leadership style. Plenty of people believe that she does not have what it takes to be a respected individual in politics, but she continuously proves them wrong by standing by her beliefs and her abilities. Through her success, many women have found great inspiration.

She admits that it can be scary to think about all of the ways that others are willing to work against her, simply because they want her to fail. This was a feeling that could have either made or broken her career. She chose the former, deciding to use their harsh words as more fuel added to her fire. Without slowing down, Ocasio-Cortez has become an icon for female empowerment all over the world. So many people look up to her because of her unwillingness to mold to the stereotypes that are being placed in front of her.

Being fearful of your own success sounds trivial, but it can become a huge hindrance to your career. When you are told the same things over and over again, it is only a matter of time before you start to believe them. As women are placed in boxes that try to determine what they are and are not capable of, it can sometimes seem easy to just go along with the narrative that is already laid out in front of you. Know that change begins on a small scale, though. While you might not be able to change the opinions of those around the world, you can show the people around you what you are made of.

Confront the very core of your fear. For example, you might worry that your new leadership position will come with longer and less forgiving working hours. What will happen if you have to work more? Many women fear losing quality time with their loved ones, which is a valid concern. In breaking down your fears, you will see that you aren't necessarily afraid of the additional work that must be put in, but instead, the time that might be lost with your family. When you have this knowledge, you will be able to work on your personal life/work life balance. Knowing when you have to work will make it easier to know when you will have time for your family. If you place a priority on both, you will be able to manage both.

A lot of fear is based on the idea of failure. To boost your morale, focus on your accomplishments. What have you already been successful at in your career? These milestones will allow you to boost yourself with the confidence that you need. Failure is always going to be an option, but this doesn't mean that it has to stop you from what you are doing. Don't count yourself out before you even begin. By reminding yourself of what you are capable of, you will be able to show others the same strengths and courage. When you stop your fears from getting the best of you, this will allow you to feel that you are more in control of the outcome.

Acknowledge that your success is not only a way to prove that you are good enough, but it can also be a way to change lives. The things that you do will directly impact other people. Many great leaders enjoy their accomplishments so much because they can see that other people are benefitting from them. If you cannot find the strength within to reach your goals, don't forget to consider the other people that will be touched by your work. No matter what industry you are in, what you are doing matters.

You aren't going to be able to work through your fears overnight, but the process can begin immediately. By having a desire to overcome your fears, you are already proving that you are stronger than them. You do not need to live your life ruled by the forces you cannot change. Instead, look to the things that are constants, like your ability to work hard for what you want. If you don't give up on these things, your hard work is surely going to pay off. Understand that you need to be easy on yourself sometimes. You are going to get stressed out and this is natural, but the way that you handle your stress is the important part.

Breaking the Glass Ceiling

Even in this era, a glass ceiling still exists for women. Because it is not discussed or officially defined, it is easy for others to argue that no such thing exists. The fact is, women are presented with these opportunities that look equal to those given to men, but they are not. There are still barriers in place that clearly suggest that women are not meant to be in high leadership positions, even when they are fully capable of being there. Because of this, you need to be aware that you might have to take on the hardship of breaking through your own glass ceiling in your given industry. You not only need to prove yourself worthy of the position, but you must also be able to motivate yourself to keep pushing past the glass ceiling. The position you want might be beyond it.

The easiest way to break through is by not listening to the hype that surrounds your desired position. As long as you are able to home in on the facts, you will be able to remain focused. Don't become psyched out because others are describing your position as unattainable or unrealistic. Only you know what you are truly capable of, so you should be the one who decides what is and is not possible. By ignoring the chatter that can surround high-level positions, you are already taking one step toward breaking through the glass ceiling. You are showing others that you are not going to let opinions stop you from showcasing your full potential.

Sometimes, when you need more challenges, you must create them for yourself. Your bosses might express to you that your options are limited, but when you know that you can strive for more, you still need to show this. Positions might be pushed in your direction that distract you from the position that you truly want. Those who want the power to stay a certain way will often offer these jobs as a way to make it appear that they are being inclusive. In reality, they might be avoiding offering you the job that you really want because they are hoping that you will settle for the one that was already offered. Sometimes, it can seem easier to settle. It is a more direct path, but if it isn't what you really want, then you should not have to settle for anything less.

When you live your life as though you are not limited, you will be able to make decisions based on your true desires. Go for the job that you really want and show everyone that you are capable of it, even without support. It does help to know that you have a team of people cheering you on, but you don't need it. You can be your own cheerleader if you need to be. Many women go forward knowing that everyone has doubts about them, yet they are still able to succeed in high-level positions. This shows that women have a lot of courage and untapped potential. As a minority, they were driven to go above and beyond to prove their worth.

To break through the glass ceiling that you are facing, you need to raise your standards. When you complete this step first, you won't be tempted to settle for anything less. Raising your standards involves knowing your worth. Think about what you have to offer and why it is so valuable. Understand that you deserve a great salary and copious amounts of respect. Making mistakes along the way should be expected; this means that you are trying new things! Don't be afraid to admit when you have made a mistake. This shows that you have integrity and that you are willing to learn from your failures. A lot of women feel the need to cover up their mistakes or stay silent about them because they already have so much working against them. You can confidently stand behind your mistakes and show others how you plan on growing from them.

Network and collaborate freely! You do not have to wait for permission from higher-level executives to tell you that you should be forming connections with those who can help you. By using your interpersonal skills, you can create a wonderful network of professionals that can help mentor and guide you along the way. Sometimes, it helps to know these people because it will prove that you have the initiative necessary in order to succeed in the position that you are striving for. Also, by making these connections, you are not paying attention to any glass ceilings that might be in place. By working independently and striving for your goal, you are going to prove that you are motivated and determined to make it happen no matter what.

Don't forget to use all of your skills. By only paying attention to your professional knowledge, you are selling yourself short. Remember that emotional skills and personal skills are also very helpful. If you know how to talk to someone or listen to their problems, this can actually make you an even better leader. This is why it is so important that you are aware of what you are capable of. When you have a grasp on the skills that you currently have and the ones that you are working on, you should be able to enter almost any situation with confidence. Think about the women who came before you that you look up to. Did they simply sit back and listen to the unofficial rules, or did they strive harder to make names for themselves?

FIVE

The 33% Rule

I t is no secret that those you spend a lot of time with can influence you. The people who you are constantly around have the ability to impact the way that you think and act. For this reason, the 33% rule exists. Because it is thought that the top 5 people who you spend time with will end up influencing the most, you need to divide this time between a mentor, peers, and those who you can mentor/guide. When you are able to be aware of those you are spending your time with, you will see that it truly makes a difference in your career ambitions. Every single day, you should be focused on doing something that is going to improve your chances of landing your dream job. By focusing on who you'd like to spend the most time with, you are ensuring that you will be learning the right skills for your future.

While it isn't possible or fun to live your life in such a calculated manner, you can take the 33% rule as a general guideline to help you make sure that your life is balanced. Think about the people that you are currently spending the most time with. These people are likely going to be your loved ones, your best friends, and your peers. Now, consider what qualities each of these individuals brings to your life. Sometimes, this process can showcase just how many negative influences you are allowing into your life. Friends who might mean well by constantly encouraging you to get out of the house and to let loose might actually be hindering your professional progress. The same can be said for those loved ones who get mad at you when you must work late.

It is understandable that human nature would push us toward prioritizing the people we love the most, but consider that placing more of a focus on your career will actually allow you to spend more time with them in the long run. When you have a secure job that pays well, you won't have to worry about the stress of having enough money to pay your bills or buy your loved ones the items that they deserve. A lot of stress is placed on this financial aspect of life, whether you tend to be focused on it or not. It can really end up driving you apart from your loved ones because you do not want to disappoint them. Know that all of the hard work that you put into your job today is going to end up impacting your loved ones in the future. Think about how much more time you will have to spend with them if you work just a little bit harder right now to secure a better position. Anyone who truly cares about you will be able to see these benefits, too.

Spending Time with the Right People

Consider each of the people that you spend the most time with. Would you be happy and confident if you had to take on their personalities and work ethics? This is important to consider because they are each going to influence you in some way.

While you might love these people very much and enjoy spending your time with them, you need to consider what kind of influence they are having on your daily life. Those with procrastination habits can lead you to the same coping mechanisms. If you are spending time with those who do not believe in the prioritization of your work life, then you can likely conclude that they are going to influence you by pulling you away from the things that you want to be focused on.

To make sure that you are spending your time with the right people, you need to have a firm grasp on your life philosophy. These are the beliefs that you value and the things that you strive to live your life by. Even if you believe that you are set in your beliefs, remember that you are still going to converse with the people in your life. The things that you talk about have a very big chance of becoming your reality. If you only discuss negative things and constantly complain, then your life is going to be focused on these things. Keeping yourself in a negative mindset can greatly impact your ability to work and often lead you astray.

You have the ability to choose what you'd like to focus your attention on. No matter how much you care about someone and enjoy spending time with them, you might be unfairly giving more of yourself to them than you need to. If you have ever had a friendship that only consisted of the other person complaining while you listen, then you have likely begun to take on the role of this person's unofficial therapist. This is a lot for anyone to handle and it can make it seem like their problems are your problems, too. Know that you can be supportive of your loved ones without taking on their pain and hardship. When you are just a little bit guarded, you will also be able to be stronger for them.

When you get into habits with your loved ones, it can be incredibly hard to break them. A fear that you likely have is that you do not want to upset them when you say that you cannot spend as much time together or when you have the desire to do other things together. Know that these changes are necessary if you want to make sure that the relationship is healthy for both of you. Just as much as they influence you, know that you also influence them. If you are both stuck in a type of rut, then there is little hope that either one of you will be able to make the productive changes that are necessary. It takes a few weeks to form a habit, so don't feel discouraged if you don't see any progress being made. It will happen, as long as you keep working at it.

Create distance when you notice that someone is holding you back. Again, you do not have to take these people out of your life, but you can choose how much time you are spending with them. If you are experiencing negative coping mechanisms, you need to take a look at the habits of those around you. Know that it is okay to have your own standards and to take some time for yourself if you are being influenced by the bad habits of others. When you are going through this process, you can't simply raise your standards and expect other people to comply with them. Not only is this unrealistic, but it is also not your job to do.

Your social environment is very important to the success that you will see in life. When you can have a better handle on this, you will feel more prepared to take on anything that comes your way. If someone constantly shows you that their beliefs contradict your own, then you need to take this as a sign. Because it is not your job to change others' minds or try to convince them of why they should believe in your values, you need to seriously consider if they are a negative or positive influence in your life. Those who impact your life in a positive way should make you want to be a better person. They should challenge you to learn and grow while supporting you every step of the way. These people have an understanding of why you might need to distance yourself at times and they will not take it personally when you do.

Surround yourself with people that have goals of their own. Sometimes, you can be spending your time with those who are generally positive, yet unguided. This isn't always a bad thing, but it can become a burden when you are focusing on something that you'd like to accomplish and the other person cannot relate to it. This is often when feelings get hurt or misunderstandings arise. Without a focus of their own, this person is going to be a lot more reliant on you. They might even be trying to live vicariously through you. This is a lot different than someone being inspired by you. Make sure that you are aware that people who are unmotivated can end up rubbing off on you if you are not careful.

You need to assemble a team of people that you feel will best make up the 33% rule. First, think about those who fit into the mentor category. These people should be the ones who inspire you the most. They should be successful in their own right with plenty of valuable life experiences. Your mentors are the ones you should be able to turn to if you need advice or guidance. They will also be willing to listen to you when you talk about your career and your ambitions. When you are around this kind of energy, you are naturally giving yourself an advantage because you will start to model your own behavior in the same way.

The next people you must find are your peers. This is not exclusive to those you work with. You can consider your peers those individuals who are on the same level as you. Even if you have entirely different work ambitions, these are the ones who are driven and goal-oriented in their own way. When you can find commonality in the desire to reach goals, this is going to provide you with a very stable and healthy relationship to keep in your life. You should be able to discuss your hardships and your successes with this person because they will be able to relate. It is important to have people who understand you, even if they are not going through the exact same things.

The final group of people you should be spending your time with are those you feel you can help. They might provide you with other valuable traits that benefit your own life, but you also need to feel that you can provide something of value to them. Being able to mentor someone is going to give you a purpose. It will also keep you on track because it is important to keep your skills sharp in order to gain the respect that you deserve while you are taking on this mentor role. When you pay attention to the people you are choosing to spend your time with, you will realize that their influence matters. You don't need to limit yourself, but having an awareness of who you become close to is going to help you in the long run.

Supporting Others

While you are probably very familiar with what it is like to be mentored, taking on the role of a mentor yourself might be new. It is important that you seek out these opportunities because they will make you a better leader. Being someone's mentor is like a condensed version of leadership. Instead of leading an entire team, your actions are influencing a single person. In some ways, this can be even more of a responsibility because the individual is going to be looking for direct guidance from you. While you are mentoring someone, you always need to remember to display your best qualities first. These first impressions will have a big impact on what the other person learns from you.

People love to learn by viewing real-life examples. If you can show your mentee that you have been in their shoes, they are going to be a lot more willing to trust you and take your advice. Try to make yourself as relatable as possible in order to show others that they can overcome their hardships. As a mentor, it is your aim to be an inspiration. Think about what first drew you toward your mentor. What qualities do you personally look for? The following are some examples of qualities that people normally find inspirational:

- Decisive: When you are able to make a firm decision on the spot, this shows others that you have already calculated the risks. When you can do this quickly, you need to have a good sense of both logic and instinct. It can be incredibly hard to make decisions, especially when there is a deadline attached. The more that you are placed into leadership positions, the more decisions you are going to have to make. People want leaders who will be able to make decisions effortlessly, not those who are still unsure of the outcome. A leader is supposed to give the team hope of a great outcome. They typically do so by enforcing their decisions with carefully thought-out plans.
- Confident: Being confident goes hand-in-hand with leadership. As a leader, you need to believe in yourself the most. Even if no one else in the room believes in you, your own support is all that you should need in order to make your decisions and lead your team to success. People find inspiration from those who are able to remain confident while being faced with adversity. As a woman, you should be able to relate to this greatly. Use your life experiences to show others why they should never give up.

- Kind: A lot of people mistakenly believe that you cannot be a powerful force while also being kind to others. It does take a certain sense of unwavering power to become a great leader, but this does not mean that you must walk all over others to get there. You can be an excellent leader while also being a nice person; the two are not related. By remembering that other people have helped you get to where you are today, this will keep you humble. The moment that you let your humility get away from you, you will become at risk of treating people less than they deserve to be treated.

- Motivated: Everyone knows that a motivated leader is going to be a leader that gets things done. Staying motivated can be incredibly difficult, especially if you are surrounded by distractions. Keeping your focus on your goals, you should be able to work around anything that stands in your way. This is pure motivation at its finest. A lot of people realize that they are the only ones who are stopping themselves from succeeding. When you can figure out a way to teach people how to work past procrastination and distractions, you will see that you can really help them.

- Ambitious: Having ambitions means that you are not willing to only settle for what you are given. This proves that you have what it takes to be a great leader and inspiration because you are always willing to strive for more. This can be a very hard quality to learn, especially when you have been struggling with your own personal life goals. When you have the desire for more, you are always going to figure out new ways to get more. Those who are constantly working on themselves so that they can accomplish more will find themselves happier overall.

When you feel that you have all of the qualities necessary for being a great mentor, you might wonder where you will find someone who is in need of a mentor. You can think about your own journey to help you with this. Where did you find your mentor? Most people who seek professional mentors end up finding them at work. This makes sense because the individual is already going to be working in your field and will have all of the necessary experience to help you succeed. If you notice a coworker who is in need of guidance, don't be afraid to step in. This might be the beginning of your mentorship journey.

A lot of women feel conflicted about coaching their peers because they do not want to come off as bossy or controlling. This is one of the stereotypes about women that is still lingering in offices all around the world. Know that you are not being bossy if the individual is benefitting from your advice. The thing about being a mentor is that the person is only going to be responsive to you if they desire your help. You cannot force your advice on anyone unless they are receptive to it. Understand that it is not wrong for you to want to help your peers succeed. Even if you are considered to be on the same level, that doesn't mean your advice isn't going to be helpful to them. You are your own person with your own set of skills and experiences.

In order to be a great mentor, it all comes back down to your ability to believe in yourself. When you know what you have to offer, you won't be scared to step in when you see an opportunity to do so. When you support others, you are being given a chance to put your skills to the test. It is very easy to list off all the skills you believe you are great at, but being able to prove this is something entirely different. It is great to challenge yourself in this way because it will keep you honest with yourself. You will know right away if you take on more than you can handle, but this doesn't mean that you won't learn how to get there. Remember that everyone starts from the bottom. No matter how skilled you are, your starting point is going to remain the same as everyone else's. You can use this wisdom and your own experience as a way to motivate your mentee to do better and to get more out of life. This is very relatable advice for many different people.

SIX

You Can Lead, Even When You Are Not in Charge

Break free from the idea that you need to hold an important title in order to lead others. Many women tend to sit back and accept that they are not leaders just because it is not in their job description. This is how the average workplace is designed in order to keep the patriarchy in place. In today's society, more and more women are ignoring this imaginary rule and proving that they can still be great leaders from where they stand. If you have ever felt that your job title was holding you back, you can move past it. Without doing anything that is not asked of you, there are still plenty of opportunities to showcase your skills and to show others that you can be a great leader.

Speak up when you feel that something should be changed. When you have your own opinions, this shows that you are thinking like a leader. Sometimes, you might agree with the majority, but there will also be times when you believe in your own ideas more. It is okay to disagree with the people you work with, even if they are your leaders. There is no harm in sharing your ideas because they can show some new insight on the same issues. Having additional viewpoints is a very effective way to solve problems that are on a larger scale. Understand that using your voice is not a negative thing. The worst that can happen is that others will not agree with you. As long as you are confident in what you are saying, this should not be enough to deter you.

A great leader uses great judgment. Always listen to your gut instinct before you act. If you truly feel that you need to speak up or take action, then there is likely a very good reason. When you listen to your instincts, you will have facts to back up your behavior. Being able to explain what you are doing and why is a trait that any good leader should possess. It showcases an organized thought process while allowing you to prove that you have the skills it takes to make a difference. Remind yourself that you can lead if you really want to. Consider it practice for when you actually land the leadership position of your dreams.

Lead Yourself Well to Lead Others Better

"Civilization is always in danger when those who have never learned to obey are given the right to command." -Bishop Fulton Sheen

This concept is simple, but it will allow you to focus on what is most important. The way that you carry yourself is like your message to your peers. If you are put together and always prepared to do anything, then this is going to send others the message that you value your job and you have the skills that it takes to be great at it. Those who lack confidence or an organized plan are going to have to work a lot harder to show others what they are capable of. People tend to stray from leaders who can't even seem to keep themselves in line. You must always lead by example, so you need to be thinking about what the most desirable leadership qualities are and show them to those around you.

You need to have fundamentals in place that you stand by. These fundamentals are your workplace values, the things that matter to you and drive you to become better. Whether you enjoy working on social justice issues or getting large projects done efficiently, you must be able to show others that you are putting your time and energy into productivity. When you have results to show for your fundamentals, this is going to make a great impression on your peers. Not only will you be working on accomplishing these things for them, but you must also do it for yourself. By keeping your morale high, you will be able to feel proud of the work that you are doing.

If you become stagnant in the way that you carry yourself, this is only going to convey a message of laziness or an unorganized approach. As noted, people will be a lot more hesitant toward a leader who doesn't seem to have a solid plan for themselves. The way that you work and carry yourself is going to be a preview of the way that you plan on leading others. Even though it can be incredibly hard to constantly keep yourself motivated, this is your golden ticket into a leadership position. Remind yourself that this is the test you must pass before you are given the larger responsibility of managing others. Work on your productivity by always having goals to reach for. Understand that you need to push yourself harder sometimes, even when there are no deadlines pending for you.

By starting these habits early, you will be well-established by the time you must teach them to others. The more you do something, the more it becomes second nature. It makes sense to live by the same principles that you will soon be encouraging others to live by. Leaders who do not take their own advice can often be seen as dictators rather than leaders who are willing to mentor. Giving commands is only a very small part of being a leader. You need to have the conviction if you truly want people to do what you are suggesting.

Have the Courage to Act

Instead of waiting for someone to give you instructions to act, you can provide yourself with the initiative that you need. In order to be a great leader, you should take a look at each situation and determine where you can best contribute the skills that you have. By getting into this kind of mentality, leadership is going to come naturally to you. Think about all of the struggles that you have already overcome at this point in your career. As a woman, you have likely been treated differently at work because of others doubting your skills or your abilities. Use this to fuel you and give you courage. Remember all of the obstacles that you had to work around to prove yourself as worthy of being there.

Being able to take action on your own requires guidance. You can get this guidance from a mentor or others who inspire you. If you feel that you need some more inspiration in your life, use the resources around you. There are plenty of books and movies that cover the topics of great leadership that can provide you with ideas for how to become a leader yourself. Inspiration isn't always going to be apparent, which is why you need to seek it. Those who settle into their habits without the desire to learn do not usually become leaders because following seems to be more comfortable.

Be the woman that little girls can look up to and feel inspired by. Show these girls that anything is possible, regardless of gender, race, or age. When all of these things are stripped away, all that matters are the skills that you have and how to use them. Think about what your younger self struggled with the most. What can you presently do that can help others who are currently going through the same thing? When you use your leadership abilities to help others, you are going to keep the momentum going for women's rights. This is very important because it takes strong leaders to persist, even in the face of doubt.

Work on your fears as best as you can. By now, you should easily be able to identify them and think about different methods that you can use to move past them. When your fears aren't holding you back, your courage will be able to shine. You might have to go through a process of trial and error while you attempt to use your courage, but this is how you are going to learn. Making mistakes is not the end of the world — everyone makes them! Understand that you can learn from them and correct them. Without completely hindering you, your mistakes can become very valuable tools.

In the moments when you wonder if you should speak up or do something, the answer is almost always going to be yes. This is how you are going to be able to push yourself out of your comfort zone. Alternatively, when you really feel like saying no, you should say yes. This is how you are going to combat laziness and any kind of stagnant attitude. Breaking free of your bad habits is going to show you that you are capable of making courageous decisions.

Be Obnoxious About How Values-Driven You Are

Sometimes, boasting is necessary. As a woman in the workplace, you were likely taught to never brag about yourself and never speak of the things that you believe you are great at. This type of behavior is often classified as "stuck up" or "being full of yourself." Women are often given these labels because men are threatened by their accomplishments. Don't let this deter you from talking about yourself. Having pride is not a negative quality, as long as you don't let it get in the way of how you learn and grow. Make it a point to tell and show others what your values are at all times. Your values make up who you are as a person and as a businesswoman. It is definitely okay for you to remind others about your values because you should be proud of them.

You can change the entire culture of your company by the way that you are able to freely express your values. When a company is able to adopt a values-driven approach, its consumers will feel that they are representing a worthy cause. This can be great for business and it will also establish a great reputation for the company. In order to start this process, a leader must be open about their own values. You can be this person, the leader who inspires others to work based on values and beliefs.

A great example of a company that has taken a values-driven approach is the fish market in Pike Place. Known for its bustling atmosphere and world-famous shopping, the fishmongers at Pike Place have become a landmark for anyone wanting to experience true Seattle culture. Their philosophy revolves around the idea that customers are treated like old friends. Their friendly employees will always make you feel like you are welcome, no matter how many times you have been there. The owners of the company noticed that people were happier when they were treated this way. In return, they started buying lots of fish!

The main quality that the fishmongers value is kindness. There is nothing complicated behind it or deceiving in the way that they treat their customers. By simply being nice to one another and having fun each day, they have created a one-of-a-kind atmosphere that keeps the market one of the busiest in the world. This all started because of the way that the employees approached their work. They could have chosen to remain stiff and professional, but think about what that would have meant for the future of the fish market.

It only takes a little bit of influence to create a huge change. Their culture blossomed successfully because the employees were acting on their genuine feelings. This was something that they all believed in enough to adopt into their everyday routines. Imagine what you could do for the culture of your own company by acting as genuinely as possible. When you are able to showcase your beliefs while also doing a great job at your work, this is how real change starts.

Understand that Power Isn't Everything

Leadership is often paired with power. The two typically become associated because leaders must be able to influence other people and make the best decisions on behalf of the entire team. Being aware of the differences between leadership and power will help you gain the respect that you deserve. You do not need to bully others into submission in order to get them to listen to you. A mistake that aspiring leaders often make is focusing too much on the power that they have over others and failing to realize how this impacts the work environment. Remember, a healthy work environment is essential to any great business venture.

A great example of leadership without overuse of power can be seen through the "Greta Effect." Named after Greta Thunberg, 15-year-old activist, the concept stems from her ability to make a worldwide difference on the topic of climate change by inspiring multi-city protests that were led by students. Starting with a protest herself, Greta silently began the revolution that impacted not only her home country of Sweden but those around the world who were watching her. Requesting that the government respond radically to climate change, Greta made her point with her consistency.

In order to state her message, Greta did not shout it from rooftops or spend a lot of energy trying to convince her peers why she was right. Instead, she turned inward and relied on her confidence and determination to fight for a cause that she truly believed in. This displayed an amazing sense of power that she gracefully used in order to fight for what she believed was right. Other people were able to hear her message loud and clear, even as she was silently sitting on the steps of the parliament building in Stockholm. Her energy was non-threatening, but it displayed so much confidence and bravery. Many of the world's top leaders were able to recognize that this young girl had a lot of power behind her stance.

Stories such as this one continue to prove that women and girls around the world have a lot to say. No matter how the message is stated, there can be a lot of power present. It all depends on how confident you are regarding your own beliefs. When you can look anyone in the eyes and explain why you feel the way that you do about important issues, then you likely have a cause that is worthy of following. You don't always have to overpower other people in order to make them see things your way. Instead, you can lead by example. Provide them with the facts and examples that they never even realized they needed.

The next time that you are feeling down on yourself because you believe that you are not powerful, consider the influence that you already have. Think about how you can use your voice without even speaking. These actions that you can showcase will become an extension of your power. By learning how to harness it correctly, you will find that you are actually much more confident than you realized.

3 Strategies for Female Managers

1. Over-Communicate: Women are already naturally inclined to communicate clearly, but this strategy will allow you to get rid of almost every opportunity to be misunderstood while at work. Not only should you be very clear about what you expect from your team and what you would like them to do, but you should also explain to them why it matters to you. When they are able to hear it from you, it is going to sink in. Without being repetitive, you can explain to them how these tasks align with your values and how you believe that their completion can benefit the entire company. Women who lead this way are often seen as very transparent bosses. Your peers will be more likely to confide in you when you are transparent in this way. As a communicative boss, your goal should be to make your employees feel that they are working for a cause, not just a paycheck.

2. Ban "Bossy:" When young girls are growing up, the term "bossy" is often tossed around. Bossy has been used negatively for the last several decades, suggesting that females who are given the title must be viewed in a negative light. This type of stereotype is sexist because boys can behave the exact same way, yet they are rewarded for being great leaders. You can change this narrative. If anyone calls you bossy in the workplace, correct them by explaining why you are so driven and motivated. Show them that you are aiming to reach these goals for a reason, not just to order people around. Your actions all have a purpose behind them, so you should not let others determine your cause. To reinforce your point, eliminate the word "bossy" from your

vocabulary. Create a reason for people to listen to you other than the idea that you want to tell them what to do.

3. Leverage Your Gender: While your gender has worked against you in the workplace for so long, you can actually use it to propel you forward in the workforce. Now that you know the distinct differences between the ways that men and women lead, you can use these differences as strengths that will work to your advantage. Use your emotional expression to fight for your cause, giving people the motivation to work harder. Allow your communication skills to guide you toward the people that you need to be interacting with, opening more doors for you and your team. Show others that the way your brain organizes and categorizes information can come in handy, allowing you to see things from a new perspective. You no longer have to think about your gender as a setback or a hardship. Instead, think of it as a blessing. Others already have certain expectations of you, so show them why these expectations are correct and, in fact, totally beneficial. Prove them wrong by showing them what you are made of.

SEVEN

Collaboration Over Competition

There is so much focus placed on women in leadership that the message often becomes lost in translation. Instead of women working together in order to reach goals and create successful outcomes, there is a sense of competition that gets brought forward. While there is nothing wrong with having a little bit of healthy competition in the workplace to keep you motivated, you must remember that other women are fighting some of the same battles that you are. If you cannot support one another, then you are both just working in vain at getting rid of these unfair expectations that are constantly being placed on women. Understandably, it can be hard to work with others who are considered your direct competition, but this type of work ethic can actually get you further in your career than you realize.

This chapter will focus on the ways that you can support others through collaboration. Instead of only allowing one person to lead at a time, you can come together with your leadership efforts in order to create a better result. Collaboration happens in every single workplace, allowing for some amazing ideas and growth to form. If you are interested in taking your leadership skills one step forward, you must learn how to successfully collaborate with those around you. By getting rid of your ego and switching your focus to the goal at hand, you will be able to see that there are many different ways to get a successful result while being inclusive of those around you with the skills that you need.

Women Who Support Women Are More Successful

Understand that your coworkers should be your allies, not your enemies. It does not make sense to work with others that you do not value or get along with because this factor will always stand in your way, no matter how hard you are personally willing to work. Being able to get along with your peers is just as important as being a fair leader. As you are working hard to earn a leadership position, those who are above you are going to be paying attention to how well you work in a team setting. You must be able to work just as hard for your team as you work for yourself. This is a judgment of character, one that is very important to those who are evaluating you.

When you are trying to get ahead in your career, you must remember to look at the bigger picture. If you are showing your bosses that you are able to work hard, yet you have a difficult time working with others, this is going to be a big setback for you. Anyone who wants to be a great leader must realize that they are going to rely on their team from time to time. No one gets to the top all on their own. It is with the help of other people who are skilled that you are going to be able to move forward as a whole. For this reason, you should always do your best to support other powerful women who work hard.

If you see a fellow woman struggling, think about the ways that you can help her succeed. Without sacrificing your own position, there are likely many things that you can do to uplift her while simultaneously showing your support. Leaders who are willing to help others are seen as humble. As you know, being known as humble is a great trait to hold onto. There are so many people in leadership positions who are so self-focused that they do not even realize when their actions are impacting others. Operating this way is only going to create conflicts and distrust.

There is always going to be power in numbers. Think about all that you will be able to accomplish with a powerful team of women. The skills that women possess in the workplace will be doubled and tripled when you can find ways to come together and use those skills to the advantage of the entire group. Many women who are too focused on competition forget that not everything has to be a fight. When you are further isolating yourself from other women in the workplace, you are going to be working extra hard when you really don't need to. Try to embrace the idea that you can all work together while still showcasing your unique skills and ideas.

If you want to work well with anyone, you need to get to know them. Instead of seeing your fellow women peers only for their skills or what they have to offer at work, try to understand them on a personal level. You don't need to make a bunch of new best friends at work, but getting to know one another will definitely help you work better together. As you form this connection, the other women are also going to be getting to know you. Having an understanding of one another on a more personal level will eliminate a lot of the conflict and bantering that might have come up before. There is a delicate balance between getting to know someone and keeping the relationship professional. You can do both if you put in the effort.

Understand that men and women need different kinds of networks to succeed. A study has shown that female leaders in top positions are often better-equipped with a close circle of fellow female contacts. Whether these contacts consist of other female leaders or those who have a lot of knowledge to offer, it can be very beneficial to have this tight circle around you. These women can provide you support when you are in need. They will also be there for you to bounce ideas off of. Men tend to focus their networking on centrality. If they are centrally located, they believe they will have access to the best jobs and opportunities. For this reason, men typically will not try to seek out friendships when they network. Instead, they stick close to what they know.

The most successful women usually keep both centrality and personality in mind. While staying close to those who are important, women are often also willing to go the extra mile and befriend other women who have nothing to offer them or their careers. This combination ensures that women are more open when it comes to networking and letting others get close to them. When women have this sense of duality, it makes them feel more motivated and able to succeed in the workplace. Because of the unique challenges that only women face, it really helps to be able to talk to others who can relate on a personal level.

Men typically see venting as a sign of weakness, especially to their peers. Instead of talking about the issues that bother them, they will tend to keep them bottled up. Women can really benefit from other women because these conversations are very healthy to have. In talking about the issues that are impacting them, women are able to come up with different ways to fight the adversity that they must face.

Collaborating in the Workplace

With a mindset that is focused on teamwork, you are going to be the most successful version of yourself. As you know, being able to work with others is a very valuable skill. It is one that shows you are flexible enough in your opinions to make changes, yet you still have ideas of your own. By improving your collaboration skills, you are going to be an even more powerful force in the workplace. The following are some real ways that you can bring the focus onto collaboration and teamwork in your own workplace:

- 3-Step Onboarding: This is a practice that can help new employees find their places in the company. From the very first day, a new employee will be given an experienced employee to shadow. This person is responsible for helping the new employee with integration. After some time shadowing this person, the new employee will be assigned several others to shadow. This will show them all of the different approaches that can be taken at the job, eliminating the idea that there is only one right way to do something.

The next step comes during projects or group tasks. By putting together teams of people who have yet to work together, or who have had minimal experience working together, everyone gets to mingle a little bit. Getting used to working with every member of your team is super important. It will keep you versatile and able to work on your flexibility. The final step of this process comes when leaders of these teams must be assigned. With a rotating leadership schedule, everyone will get the chance to lead, even the newest employees. This will give everyone a way to practice their skills and also experience different leadership styles.

- Role-Switching: This strategy is exactly as it sounds — two employees with different roles switch places for a day. During this process, both people will gain an appreciation for the job that they are placed in. Without knowing exactly what your peers go through on a daily basis, it can be hard to relate to their struggles. When you are experiencing it first-hand, you will realize that they might be going through entirely different tasks and stressors than you are. This kind of switch in perspective is great for every employee. When you are able to have more respect for one another, you are automatically going to work a lot better together.
- Unconventional Business Meetings: Going through the same old work meetings can be draining and mundane. If possible, change up the way that your team meets. While keeping some of the standard meetings in place to cover the important topics, you can change the structure of your other meetings in order to provide a more relaxed approach. If you are a meeting leader, you can have your employees meet somewhere other than a conference room to discuss your roster of topics. A simple change in the environment can do a lot for the team's morale. You can also select different people each meeting to lead the entire thing. When you do not have to make the same speeches and statements over and over again, the meeting is going to feel a lot more lively.

You can also try to schedule meetings that aren't necessarily for the purpose of discussing work. Having clubs in the workplace that still allow employees to meet, but in a more casual way, has proven to be very beneficial. Everyone gets to know one another and they will have fun while doing so. Starting a Lunch Club, where you eat lunch together once a month, can be a great way to let everyone mingle while still having a sense of teamwork behind the action. By making a commitment to joining a work club, each employee is saying that they care about teamwork.

- Peer Recommendations: Receiving feedback is very important to your growth as an employee. It is not only great to get feedback from your supervisors, but it can also be beneficial to know what your team thinks about you. By starting the habit of giving each other compliments, you can get to know what strengths others see in you. Known as "peer recommendations," try to incorporate them into your regular meetings. Each person will go around and mention one team member who they feel has really stepped it up for the week. They can explain what skills this person has that they feel are valuable and why they selected this person.

Not only is this a big morale booster, but it helps when a team can say kind things about their other team members. This will allow you to feel that you are a part of something that is close-knit. When you have this kind of security, you will be more motivated to work hard and go the extra mile because you know that your team is always going to have your back. Those who work on teams that feel divided or cold are going to be more hesitant when it comes to putting their best work forward.

- Team Traditions: Building your workplace culture is a fun and easy way to maintain a sense of teamwork. By creating traditions that are to be celebrated regularly, this gives all of the employees a sense of comradery. Whether you schedule a hangout every week or a special way to celebrate birthdays in the office, these little things are going to bring you all closer together.

Having these traditions will make the workplace less stiff and serious. While it is necessary to buckle down and work hard sometimes, it is also important to understand that you are all just human beings with different things going on in your lives.

Collaborating in Your Personal Life

The way that you are either willing or unwilling to collaborate at work can have a big impact on your personal life. What many people do not realize is that having an unhealthy competitive nature can be detrimental to all aspects of your life. If you are in a relationship, this competitiveness will often become the way that you treat your significant other. Instead of working together as partners, you might begin to experience jealousy or negativity when you see your significant other succeeding. Understandably, this can place a huge divide between the two of you. Conflicts are bound to arise and you will be left feeling unhappy.

In the same way that you try to be open to collaborating at work, you should apply these methods to your personal life. Instead of seeing yourself as the direct competition of your partner or loved ones, you should think about ways that you can work together in order to accomplish the same result. What you must remember about your personal life is that no one is trying to put you down in order to get ahead. The workplace can be very cutthroat, especially when promotions or promises of bigger salaries are involved. In general, your personal life should be a lot more relaxed in this sense. Instead of seeing your loved ones as obstacles you must work around, you need to think of them as allies. Know that anyone who truly loves you is going to want what is best for you.

If you realize that you are letting your competitive nature take over control, you can do several things to turn it around. First, understand that your loved ones might push you, but they will be doing so in order to help you grow. The ones who really care about you are always going to be willing to help you. What you might have to express to them are the ways that they can help you most effectively. Receiving a lot of constructive criticism from someone in your personal life can be very triggering. While the person might be telling you these things because they believe it can help you, their words might lead you to feel that you aren't good enough. Keep in mind that you do not always have to take the advice that is given to you. Much like in the workplace, constructive criticism is there for you to listen to. The actions that you take are your own responsibility. When you feel that your loved ones are being too hard on you, speak up about it.

Communication is the key to maintaining any healthy personal relationship. When you can communicate why you are struggling, you will be able to provide your loved ones with some insight. Lashing out at them or taking on a competitive nature is only going to fuel the tension further. Try to think about ways that you can work together rather than seeing yourselves as two separate entities. For example, if your spouse can see that you are struggling with your patience and they offer you some advice, listen to what they have to say. If you disagree, explain why you feel differently. Discussing the same topic from two different perspectives can be essential for both of you to grow. After you discuss why you have differing opinions, see if you can come together with a strategy that allows both of you to improve. Maybe your partner needs to be more understanding of your boundaries and maybe you need to try your partner's suggested techniques of staying calm under pressure. The ways that you can collaborate in your personal life tend to be much more complex, but they are just as relevant.

You can learn a lot from those who have different opinions, especially your loved ones. They have a unique set of knowledge that your coworkers might not have — they know you on a personal level. Because of this, they might be better able to understand the things that trigger you or the things that make you stressed out. It can be a humbling experience to learn what those closest to you have to say about the way that you live your life. Try to take each piece of advice with a grain of salt, remembering that you do not have to make any changes unless you find them necessary.

Show your loved ones that you appreciate them because, most of the time, they are only making suggestions to you because they want to see you do even better than you are already doing. Understand that they do not see you as a failure just because there are things that they feel you can do better. Collaborate with them by having an open dialogue of communication, being patient as they explain why they feel the way that they do. When you are open to the potential of change, this is going to make you a more well-rounded person. Remember that you can also make suggestions to your loved ones about the ways that they can improve. Couples who are willing to help one another grow in this way are not only stronger, but they are also better able to understand ideas that come from other perspectives.

EIGHT

Find Your Voice and Own It

There is so much power behind the way that you convey your thoughts. You can use your voice for many different purposes, and it can be a huge boost in self-esteem when you realize that people are willing to listen to you. Those who own their voices tend to be a lot more confident in anything that they set their minds to. Getting to this point can prove to be a challenge, but it is one that is worth taking on. In order to find your voice, you need to be aware of the things that you truly believe in. By having a concrete set of values, you will be able to speak up in any situation that requires you to. Even when you are not being put on the spot, speaking up because you feel that you have something important to say is a very empowering feeling. A lot of women tend to hold back in the workplace because they are taught that their opinions matter less. It is time to get rid of this idea and redefine the way that you communicate.

No matter what you say or do, you must remember to stay true to yourself. It is going to serve you well when you remain firm in your beliefs. Those who completely model themselves after their mentors will often lose sight of who they actually are. There is a sense of balance that must be kept when you are learning from someone else. Take their skills and listen to the knowledge that they are willing to share, but apply it to your own life. You need to be able to make your own decisions and come to your own conclusions, regardless of what others think you need to do. There is a lot of power in this process and it can even lead you to make new discoveries about yourself.

How to Stand Up for Yourself Without Hurting Your Team

Finding the balance between pleasing those you work with and still remaining firm in your beliefs can be difficult. Because there is such a fine line that you do not want to cross, you might feel like you are holding yourself back at work. This is normal, especially for women who work in male-dominated environments. One wrong move and you will be labeled as hard to work with or selfish. While these labels might be untrue, they can still hurt your reputation. As a woman who desires the same respect that men get in the workforce, there are some unique challenges that must be faced. You need to prove to everyone that you aren't a push-over, but you must do so in a way that doesn't directly challenge anyone else. The process can be maddening, often enough to push you to your breaking point.

The first step comes from the language and tone that you use. When you are communicating your point, you need to be very clear about what you mean. This can seem blunt if you are not used to communicating this way, but it is going to allow you to express yourself with minimal room for others to misunderstand you. Holding back and not providing enough clarity can confuse those that you work with. You might say one thing but really mean another thing. Say what you mean the first time and do so without pointing any fingers of blame. For example, if you feel that your work environment could use some improvement, make your suggestions directly. Explain why you feel this way and what you feel can be done about it. Unless there is a big injustice occurring, you do not have to expand on *who* you feel is causing the issues. Sometimes, no one is even at fault.

Your next step will come from learning how you can stand your ground without deliberately upsetting others. Know that you feel the way that you do for a reason. Your feelings are just as valid as any of your peers'. Women often make the mistake of putting their feelings second in the workplace because they do not want to be deemed as unlikable. If you realize that there is something happening to you that is thought to be unfair or not right, you need to say something about it. Again, without pointing fingers, you can go to your superiors and express what is happening to you. Tell them how this makes you feel and why you believe it should be changed. Understand that any healthy work environment is going to come with people who care about your well-being.

When standing up for yourself, there are certain strategies that should be avoided. Do not put yourself on a pedestal. Just as you can understand that your feelings are valid, know that others are going to have their own feelings. You are not better than your peers, so you should never act like your opinion is the only correct one. There might be several "right" opinions in any given situation. Be willing to listen actively; you just might learn something new. Instead of trying to prove to others why your opinion is better, show them why you believe in it so much. Give them as many concrete examples as you can without putting anyone else down. This is a very admirable trait for any employee to have. It shows a rational way of thinking while still showcasing that you have strength and belief in yourself.

Avoid getting into frequent conflicts with your peers. When you find that you disagree with someone else's behaviors or opinions, the way to solve this is not by agitating the situation and picking it apart. Instead, you can have a mature conversation about it in an attempt to see where that person is coming from. If this does not fix the issue, you can take it to someone who can act as a mediator. A person who is not directly involved in the situation will be able to provide unbiased insight. Know that this person might side with your peer, but at least they will be able to give it some thought in a way that is impartial to you both. Being able to stand down when you are proven wrong is something that you will learn by practicing. No one likes to admit that they were wrong, but it shows a sense of humility.

Finally, work on your ability to compromise. You probably have the most experience with this by finding middle ground with your significant other when you disagree with them. The same concept can be applied in the workplace. Understand that neither one of you might be right about an issue, but there are still ways that you can make the situation right by finding a middle ground. You are going to have to make sacrifices sometimes, but when you can find a solution that allows you to compromise, this is going to create a healthy working environment. It is also going to show others that you are willing to think about situations outside of your own opinions. It is not always about being right or wrong, but more so about doing what is best for the company.

The Power of Words

It is no secret that your words hold great power. Having an understanding of why can help you out as a female leader. No matter what position you are trying to obtain, others are going to look up to you as you begin to climb the corporate ladder.

Your actions are going to be placed under a microscope, making the way that you carry yourself more important than ever. Being able to evaluate what you are going to say before you say it can save you from having conflicts and getting into disagreements with your peers. As a leader, you need to be able to find the right balance between opinionated and offensive. While still being a likable fixture at your job, you must also be able to stand your ground when necessary.

The most important concept that you must follow when you are communicating is to take a breather before you launch into an angry or frustrated narrative. Thinking before you speak can save you a lot of time that would be spent arguing or not getting along with your peers. Again, you don't automatically have to agree with the majority because this is what women in the workplace have been fighting against for many years now. Instead, turn your focus inward. When you disagree with someone, take a few deep breaths and try to consider both opinions. Make sure that you are considering the facts that back up your own opinion. Instead of relying on the fact that you just agree with it, think of concrete reasons why it makes sense.

When thinking about the other person's opinion, try to do the same thing. Think about the supporting details that back it up. Any great leader would be able to join a debate for either team at any time; this is how to make sure that you are using your skills in a fair way. When you have a better understanding of how the other person is thinking, you might also realize certain aspects of their personality. Some people are more timid while others love to argue. There are those who are willing to submit to a superior and others who would rather put up a fight. Being a woman in leadership, you are going to be dealing with many different personality types.

You must learn how to speak to everyone. Direct conversations about issues do not always work. Some people are going to be receptive to this approach and will respect you, while others might take this as a challenge and will react by resisting. You need to assess each situation as one that is unique. Try to work through the conversation in ways that you feel the person would be most responsive to. It does not always have to include guesswork. You have the right to ask the other person how they believe the situation should be handled. This strategy usually works very well for those who are especially stubborn or opinionated.

Even when you are not in conflict, you must understand that your words hold a lot of power. What you say directly represents what you believe in. This means that anything you say off the record is also going to be considered a statement that you believe in. For example, those who engage in workplace gossip are going to be seen as untrustworthy. When a leader is willing to talk about other people's lives, this shows that they would be willing to talk about anyone. Be careful with these little nuances because they say a lot about your communication style. As a general rule, you should not discuss someone if they are not in the room. This rule applies to business and for your personal life, as well. When you can practice this in all aspects of your life, it will become a good habit that you can quickly adopt.

When modeling your communication style, think about the ways that you would like to be talked to. Harshness does not always make the best point. Sometimes, you need to take a more down to earth approach. Remember, you do not have to overpower someone in order to get their respect. By being yourself and showing that you are wise, others are going to naturally gravitate toward you. Being great at communication takes a lot of work and patience. If you are willing to give up quickly, you might never find the style that works best for you. Remember, it can take a lot of trial and error.

Remember that the way you talk to yourself can also make a huge impact on how you feel. If your inner voice is full of negativity and disdain, you are likely going to be a leader who feels that they do not deserve to be there. Any time you feel yourself slipping up and using negative language, replace these words with something positive. The sooner you are able to help yourself by being uplifting, the sooner you are going to become a great leader. Enable yourself by paying yourself compliments and using positive language. Remember that there are already so many people and factors working against you that you should not also be a part of the list. Tell yourself every single day that you deserve to be there.

Branding Yourself

You are probably most familiar with the term "branding" when it comes to social media. Self-proclaimed social media influencers boast a personal brand in order to work with companies and sell products. The idea of personal branding has become very popular in the last few years, giving people a chance to portray themselves exactly how they want to be seen by the public. Now, branding is not only relevant to influencers. It has become an integral part of nearly anyone's life. When you can brand yourself before others brand you, this is your chance to reclaim exactly what you represent and what you believe in. No matter what industry you work in, it is important to establish these things. The following are some steps to be taken in order to make sure that you are sending those you work with the right message:

- Develop Your Personal Story: Everyone has a unique backstory. This consists of all the events that led them to the present moment. When thinking back on your life and all that you have experienced so far, what stands out the most? Think about the things that have shaped you most and the things that make you the great leader that you are today. When asked about your background, you should be able to provide a single phrase to people that you feel best represents you. It can be difficult to condense your life experience into only one phrase, but it makes for an impressive moment when you are able to sum yourself up like this when asked. Of course, you can provide the long version of the story, but it is also essential to be able to have a short version. Make it clear and concise.

- Use All Forms of Communication: You now know how to find your voice, but understand that your words aren't the only way you are communicating. Being an active listener is another positive form of communication that you should showcase whenever possible. When you can listen to others and understand them, this shows that you are paying attention. The way that you dress and present yourself also becomes a part of the way you communicate. Each day, remember that your outfit can also make a statement. Dress in a way that conveys the message you are trying to send to others. When people see you speaking, listening, and dressing a certain way, this is what makes up your brand. The more consistent that you can be, the more respect and trust you will earn.

- Invest in Yourself: Keeping up with the trends is an important aspect of being a respected leader. If you only pay attention in the beginning, you are going to be left behind. Make sure that you are constantly doing research on what is popular in the workforce and what is relevant in your given industry. By being aware of your own personal brand and the values that you hold close to you, this is going to allow you to remain true to yourself at all times. The times change very quickly, so being on top of what is considered relevant will show that you are constantly willing to put in work.

- Keep Promises: This is a very important aspect of your personal brand. When you think about those who hold positions of power, how many of them would you expect to keep a promise? This can sound trivial, but it usually matters a great deal to people. If you tell someone that you are going to do something, you must always follow through. If you don't believe that you are going to make it happen, then you should not make any promises. This keeps you transparent with those you are in charge of and it also shows that you have a sense of integrity. People enjoy being heard. There is nothing that breaks this trust faster than being the recipient of a broken promise.

- Define Your Audience: When you have a personal brand for yourself, you must also have a target audience. Think about what kind of attention you would like to attract and from whom. The people that you consider your audience should be people that you can see yourself working with. Do your actions and words convey that you would like to work with these people? It can be interesting to think about things from this perspective and it can help you when you are trying to define your personal brand. A good leader is nothing without a good audience to back them up. You are going to make an impact on these individuals, so it is important that you are sending them the right messages.

Developing your own personal brand can take some time. You might work for years at coming up with the perfect representation of who you are. Understand that your brand can change. As you grow as a leader, you might realize that you'd like to convey a different message or represent something else. In doing so, this requires you to change your focus. Make sure that your personal brand reflects your most current set of values and principles. If you change this too much, people are going to become confused with the direction that you are going in.

NINE

Building a More Diverse and Inclusive Workplace

D iversity and inclusion are two of the main things that women fight for in the workplace every single day by showing up. To work for a diverse company means that you are being given the opportunity to be there. Inclusion takes this one step further. When a company is inclusive, this means that you should be given chances to work in high positions, compete for top titles, and lead others along the way. While so many companies promise that they are both diverse and inclusive, many women are disappointed to find that they are only going through the motions. There are countless times when women are promised these things, yet they are only being brought onto the team to enhance the company's statistics. Women will often work lower-level positions with no promise of promotion in order to make the company appear that they are being inclusive of all.

In this chapter, you will learn the importance of being included. Not only are you going to see how you must fight for diversity every single day, but you will also learn practical applications of how to make it happen. Women have been fighting for these things for decades and there is no end in sight. When more women in the workplace become aware of the issues that are still being faced, they will be able to come together and fight for the cause. As an empowered and informed woman, this change can begin with you. By networking with other women you work with, you have the opportunity to start a movement. Keeping this fairness in place will allow you all to feel that you have an equal opportunity to land the same jobs and work the same tasks that the men on your team can.

Diversity and Inclusion 101

Knowing the differences between diversity and inclusion is important. In order to ensure that your workplace is mindful of both, you need to have a solid understanding of what each one represents. Starting with diversity, this is the understanding and acceptance of the differences that employees have. These differences can become apparent in race, gender, ethnicity, religion, sexual orientation, and disability. There can also be diversity in education level, life experiences, skill sets, and personality. As seen, there are many ways in which we can be different from one another in the workplace. A diverse work environment does not use these factors against its employees. Instead, it is able to recognize all of these differences and still provide everyone with a fair chance.

Inclusion is the act of creating a work environment that gives everyone an opportunity to participate. In doing so, the company will become more well-rounded because of all of the different perspectives that are being used. Everyone has their own unique skills to offer, no matter how unconventional. When big companies are already successful, they can sometimes become less willing to be inclusive because they know that the method they are currently using already works. This is why women have to work so hard to climb the ranks of the corporate ladder. It can be extremely difficult to convince an entire company why they should make a change when nothing appears to be broken.

By using your voice as a woman in the workplace, you will be able to make a difference in the entire way that the company views diversity and inclusivity. It can be hard to do so in a world where the two are not prioritized. While there are some laws in place that help ensure there is fairness in the workplace, there is not much else being done to make these companies follow through with their promises. Upon being hired at a new job, the company is already fulfilling its mission of being diverse and inclusive by offering a woman a position. After this point, it is up to the company's discretion whether or not they will provide you with opportunities that extend beyond the very basic ones that they must offer.

Taking a look at the statistics, a survey was done that included 300 senior executives who worked at various large companies. The topic was on diversity and inclusivity priorities. 65% of them stated that they valued diversity during the recruitment process. 35% said they prioritized diversity in the workplace. These statistics further prove the point that these companies might be playing by the rules, but overall, they are not placing a very urgent priority on diversity and inclusion. This is why it can be super frustrating as a woman in the workplace who must constantly feel that she is fighting for the position that she already has. If your superiors do not value the unique skills and perspectives that you bring, then you must work to constantly prove to them why you deserve to be there.

If you are tired of this, you are not alone. So many women are feeling fed up with the way that companies operate, inspiring them to speak up about the issues. Know that you do not have to suffer in silence. Chances are, other women you work with are also feeling the same way. This is why it is important to network and truly develop relationships with those around you. By using your power in numbers, you can make a real difference. Understanding what diversity and inclusivity are supposed to mean, you can bring these issues up with your company. Fight for your rights because, sometimes, no one else is going to be as motivated as the one who is being impacted.

Another survey done with HR executives has shown what the best diversity and inclusivity practices are. Pay attention to these and note which ones your own company follows:

- Fair treatment
- Equal opportunities
- Priority on teamwork
- Focus on innovation and creativity
- Flexibility in the way you work
- Established conflict resolution processes
- A leader who is evidently committed to diversity
- Representation for all at all levels of the company
- Training on diversity and inclusivity

While these are known as some of the best practices, they are not the only ones. There are likely hundreds more that you can think of that would make your workplace a fairer place for women and other minorities. Those who are not part of a minority do not find as much inspiration to take action. For them, the system is working well. Change is often inspired by unfair treatment. This is why women tend to be so quick to stand up for equal rights. After feeling the treatment first-hand for so long, it is no wonder that a change is going to be desired. Women are relentless when it comes to this fight, as they should be. You should always stand up for what you believe in, even when no one else is.

Consider that there are different strategies to be used in the hope of creating more diversity and inclusivity in the workplace. Depending on your current job position and the way that your company operates, you might be able to enforce some of these strategies in an effort to make your work environment better. Creating a focus on the issue at a high level (CEO/COO) is going to make the biggest impact. When you can get the biggest boss to listen to your problems, this shows that there is going to be hope for a change. There is nothing worse than fighting for a cause that your superiors do not believe in. Schedule a meeting with the leader of the entire company. Prepare a speech that is to the point, speaking on your own personal experience and why you believe there should be a company-wide change. When you can make your point and follow it up with facts, this is how you make a great statement.

Another strategy that you can apply immediately is treating all people as equals. No matter what position someone holds or what their background is, being able to treat everyone with the same respect will further promote inclusivity. This type of behavior tends to be contagious, often inspiring your peers to do the same. When you can become the leader of this type of movement, it will show that you are truly supporting the cause for all, not just for yourself. Diversity and inclusivity are not solo battles to fight. They require a lot of support from all kinds of different individuals. Staying true to the principle, this fight should be everyone's battle.

Networking is very helpful when it comes to standing up against injustice. When you can be around others who are feeling the same way that you are feeling and going through the same experiences, there is power there. By starting outreach groups and providing employees with an abundance of resources, people are going to feel less alone. Employee happiness is very important. Not only will this impact the quality of work that is done, but it also speaks for the company overall. The companies that are able to keep their employees happy are also more likely to see higher retention rates. Companies that must constantly cycle through different employees are usually doing something wrong.

If you are ready to make a difference in your workplace, start by using your voice. Speak up when you see that anyone is being biased. By staying silent, you are becoming part of the problem. Not everyone is going to have the confidence and ability that it takes to speak up. With practice, you can become a leader in the movement. Understand that you have nothing to lose, only rights to gain. Normalize being able to express yourself without any fear of consequences. It is not wrong to hope for equality in the workplace, especially because it is a place that should feel safe and fair for all.

The Impact of Women in Leadership

As a woman, you can work hard at creating a balanced workplace. Whether your company has already taken some steps toward this goal or you must inspire them to do so, remember that your voice can make a big difference. There have been many women that came before you who have had the same goal in mind. Learn about them and use their journeys as inspiration for the way that you work. Step one begins when you can learn how to recognize bias. No matter how diverse or inclusive a company claims to be, if there is bias occurring, then they are not keeping their promise. You need to be the one who calls them out on their biased thinking. Speak up and shed light on this injustice. You can also do so on a smaller level. If your peers are using a biased approach, tell them. Inform them that they can take a different approach that is more inclusive.

In order to call people out when they are being biased, you must have a great concept of what this looks like. There is a big chance that you have experienced some sort of bias against yourself since you have been working at the company. Use this personal experience to help guide you toward an approach that is fairer. There are often times when people are unconsciously biased, unaware of the fact that they are acting this way. This is no exception because it is still biased behavior. You can treat this situation just as you would with any other biased situation. The following are some strategies that you can use to help you:

- Enforce Good Processes: The process that your workplace follows can either resist or reinforce biases. A process is anything that people are used to doing. It is usually taught from the very beginning, giving employees no reason to deviate. As a woman in the workforce, you have likely been given plenty of reasons to aspire to make changes in the process. If you have ever wished that things could be different, this is your reason. Use it wisely. When you can practice fair processes yourself, this will give others an example to look up to. Showcase your process proudly and explain why you do what you do. When you have a strong voice to represent inclusivity, others are going to listen.

- Look in Front of You: If you know that your company needs help, yet you don't know where to start, then you can start by looking in front of you. Take a look at your company's daily operations. Pay attention to the way that people are chosen to complete important tasks. What is the logic behind it? Are people chosen based on their skills or are people chosen based on the leadership that they already have within the company? In order for any company to operate fairly, there must be equal opportunity. If you are noticing biases that are taking place during your daily activities, then you can guarantee that there are biases taking place at a higher level. Sometimes, the easiest way to tackle a big change is by starting from the bottom.

- Understand That There Is No Immunity: Even those who do not seem like they would ever be impacted by biased thinking can be affected. This kind of thinking does not discriminate. When it is practiced enough, it becomes normal for people. Those who are so used to taking orders and doing what they are told are going to be very susceptible to simply accepting biased thinking as their standard way of thinking. This becomes a problem, not only in the workplace but in their personal life. The way that you think and get inspiration for your actions matters a great deal. If you are always operating on a bias, this is going to hinder you. Being biased gives you the label of being an unfair and an unlikeable person. While labels do not hold much weight, they do impact your reputation.

- Become More Self-Aware: With almost anything, change starts from within. You must become the change that you wish to see. When you are mindful of your own actions, your point is going to be even more valid. To get rid of biased thinking, you have to approach every situation as fairly as possible. Understand that your actions must match your words. This provides you with consistency that is going to earn you respect. One of the easiest ways to become more self-aware is by substituting yourself into every situation. Imagine if you were anyone else in your company. Would you still feel that you are being given a fair shot? Take everyone's personal experiences into account, acknowledging that not everyone is fighting the same fight.

Now that you have a better understanding of how to tackle bias in the workplace, you should be able to get those who are on top on board. For lasting results, you need to inspire your own leaders to make changes. Encourage them to take accountability for what is happening within the company. While you can become great at spotting inconsistencies, this does not all have to fall on your shoulders. It is not your fault that the processes are biased and the methods are unfair, but you can bring this awareness to the leaders who must then take on the responsibility.

As you work on changing these processes, remember that it is best to take a long-term approach. The little changes that are made each day matter, but the ones that will make the most impact must happen when your leaders can see a reason to make a change. By shedding light on the issues that are most important to you, this will give you a chance to speak your case to your leaders. Tell them *why* you believe this should change and offer solutions that you have already come up with. This is going to show your initiative and highlight exactly how important the cause is to your own personal beliefs. Even if they do not take your exact advice, when they agree to make a change, you can feel great about knowing that you have made a difference.

Making an impact on the company you work for not only benefits you, but it also gives a voice to others who might not be brave enough to stand up for themselves. When you can create this beacon of hope for others to believe in, you are going to be responsible for improving the diversity and inclusivity of your workplace. The issue might seem like a big one to tackle, but change must start somewhere. Understand that you are a powerful woman with powerful leadership abilities. Remember that you do not have to be offered a position of leadership in order to showcase your leadership skills. Within your right, you can make a difference and use your skills to better the entire company.

The more stories that you read about women in leadership, the more you are likely going to feel more inspired to make your own changes. This is a great example of how powerful these changes can be. Think about all of those women who will hear about your story and feel inspired by you in the same way. There is no reason why the fight must stop just because people aren't saying anything. When you are able to talk to your peers, you will be able to discover what is bothering them and how they feel that they are being treated unfairly. Don't be afraid to start these conversations.

One day, you might be ready to start a company of your own. When you can practice these skills from the position that you currently hold, this is going to give you plenty of practice for whatever your future holds. Know that the only person who has the ability to limit you is yourself. If you have been continuously fighting for a fair workplace with no results, then you might have to make a difficult decision. Know that you do not have to stay at a company just because it is prestigious or has a great reputation. If there is corruption happening within that is not being corrected, then you deserve something better. Go to the places where people listen to what you have to say.

TEN

Leaving a Legacy

Your legacy is what speaks for you when you are not speaking. It is what you leave behind for people to remember you by. When you think back on what you have accomplished, are you proud of yourself? In order to make an impact on the world, professional or otherwise, you must always be aware of what your actions are saying. The causes that you support make up a large percentage of your legacy. Your aim should be to create something unforgettable that people can continue to feel inspired by. With the way that the workforce has created countless challenges for women, leaving a legacy has become more important than ever. You have the ability to change the systems that are in place to oppress women and inspire future leaders to take charge.

How to Be Unforgettable

Taking an individual look at each of these strategies, you should feel empowered to start your own legacy. By taking tips from the methods that are proven to work, you can learn how to navigate your way to the success that you deserve. After discovering what your best qualities are, you can use them to your advantage. Make people excited about what you have to say. It all starts with the passion that you put toward the final results.

Prioritize People Over Results

Understand that your team is everything. Each person who is a part of your team contributes in their own way. Whether they have unique skills or exceptional habits that focus on the success of the team, they should all matter to you. When you are seeing the results that you desire, yet you are leading a team that feels unhappy or unappreciated, you aren't succeeding. Think about how you have felt in the past: ignored or overlooked because of who you are. It can be a very discouraging feeling to watch your company succeed while you still feel that you aren't being seen for who you are and what you have to offer.

If you think about the future, what do you think your team will remember most? They might think back on the milestones that were reached, but they will be able to remember how they were treated over everything else. Working under a leader who is not considerate or caring can be a very draining experience. You wouldn't want others to feel this way about you, so it is important that you make them feel seen and heard. Get to know each person on your team as individuals rather than one big working unit. Everybody has different stories and experiences. When you can get to know them in this way, they are going to feel that they matter because you care.

Make it a point to create many opportunities for open dialogue and communication. Ask your team directly what they like about your leadership skills and what they feel could use improvement. When you are able to humble yourself enough to receive this kind of constructive criticism, you are more likely to grow as a leader. Don't be afraid of failure. If anyone has a problem with the way that you are leading, then it is worth listening to them. There are conflicts that can be resolved in simple ways if you are willing to step down and understand them. As you know, having great conflict resolution skills is very important no matter what your job description requires.

Before you move forward with any big decisions, make sure that you get the general consensus from those you are working with. If anyone does not feel good about the work that is being done, find out why. This will also keep you in check when determining if your work practices are fair. Always ask your employees and peers how they are feeling and why. The more that you are able to listen to different opinions that come from different viewpoints, the better off you will be as a woman in leadership. The greatest leaders always have time for those they work with. They do not see these conversations as a burden, but instead, a big help.

Invest Your Time and Money

Going through the motions of being a great leader is only part of the job. You have to be invested in the cause, no matter what it is. Anything that you are willing to stand for and be a part of should be something that you would easily put your time and money into. While not every goal should be seen as something you can just throw money at in order to see results, you do need to understand that the best results are seen when a leader is truly invested. The effort that you are asking for from your peers should be the same kind of effort that you are willing to put in. You are not exempt from this process just because you might hold a different rank.

This is one way in which legacies are created. By making a lasting impact, you are ensuring that your voice is going to be remembered. Remember that short-term victories might feel great at the moment, but they aren't going to hold as much weight as the long-term goals that are reached. Think about the future and consider if your efforts are going to be remembered a year from now. What about 10 years from now? Consider your leadership a lifelong commitment. Don't stop just because you have tasted a little bit of success.

An easy way to decide on the areas you need to develop will come by getting input from your peers. Ask them directly and notice patterns that arise. If an issue is prominent enough, it will usually come up more than once. When you can decide on the things that need to be improved, you can work together as a group to come up with solutions. Instead of only turning to your team to find out what is wrong, you can also turn to them with questions on how they propose they'd like to fix these issues. Don't let them do it all on their own, though. Make sure that you are also using your own ideas and giving your own input.

No matter what decision you make, you must determine if it is going to be a win-win-win. This means that it should align with your values, benefit the team overall, and give the company a chance to grow and improve. If you are ever uncertain about a decision that you must make, think about the win-win-win concept. If it only benefits some people, then it is likely not the best option to take. Use your creativity and innovation to see how you can turn the same old solutions into brand new concepts. There are always going to be ways in which you can improve on these things. When you constantly remind yourself of this, you should feel motivated and capable of making the right changes.

Connect in Person

As the world continues to grow and technology is used more than ever, it can be easy to forget that making an in-person connection with those around you is very important. Sending emails and making phone calls have likely replaced in-person meetings. With how accessible this technology is, you have likely become very used to it. Very helpful at times, technology is able to bridge the gap between yourself and those who you would normally have to make an effort to see. Where is the happy medium? When should you opt for an in-person approach over a digital one? These are the questions that you must continue to ask yourself. The conclusion that you come to will be situational.

When you are on a tight schedule, sending an email is a valid form of communication. As you know, you must make time for what is most important. If you have to secure an investor or create a business relationship that asks a lot from the other person, it is typically a good idea to create some sort of bond with them in person. It is a lot easier to say no to an email or to forward a phone call, but denying someone in person is different. Not only are you going to get to know those of importance better, you will also be able to better explain your cause. Use your conviction to get what you want.

When doing anything involving community outreach, show your face. While you can leave this up to your team to handle, it will make more of an impact when a person who holds power is willing to show up for the cause. By connecting with the community in person, this will show them that your company really stands behind its values. It makes the company seem more approachable and will show consumers that you will value them. There is nothing worse than the feeling of being treated like a number. You have likely felt like a statistic before, both in your personal life and at work. Make sure that you genuinely get to know people because you want to. Don't do it because you are supposed to.

Being able to successfully interact with other people has been a skill that has been losing popularity over the last few decades.

With apps and technology that are available at your fingertips to do the work for you, it appears that people are connecting less and less. If you want to create a lasting legacy, you need to communicate your message. Do this in person as often as you can. Even when your interactions do not require this kind of communication, do your best to include it into your values as much as possible. By reminding yourself that you do not need technology in order to be a great leader, you will find a renewed sense of confidence in your own skills and abilities.

Control Less; Empower More

Instead of aiming for taking over more control of your team, aim to empower them to make their own decisions. It can seem scary to let go of control, especially when you have been designated a leadership position. The best leaders are known for training their employees on how to work smart, though. When you don't have to worry about controlling what everyone else is doing, you will have more time to make improvements and make the company even better. People who are able to think for themselves will also be able to come up with innovative solutions to problems and new ideas. Whenever possible, encourage your team to think outside of the box.

When you have built up an empire, it can be very scary to allow others to make decisions that will either carry it forward or cause it to come crashing down. This is a risk that you must take if you want to be a great leader who leaves a legacy. If you are only acting like a control freak, this can become very stressful. All of the obstacles that you will encounter as a team are going to weigh you down. By distributing the responsibility, you must also be willing to let others call the shots. Put trust in your team and know that they will be making the best decisions they can possibly make.

Teach your team that they can take calculated risks. It can be hard to go beyond what is expected of you, but taking risks is what creates legacies. By deciding to go beyond what you know, you will be able to experience real growth. Playing it safe feels good, but taking risks that pay off feels great. When you have an entire team of people that believe in this philosophy, you are always going to have an enjoyable work environment. Stagnant activities become boring. It takes a little bit of improvisation in order to keep things interesting.

When you take less control of your employees, this encourages them to become more independent. It takes a sense of independence to solve problems. Your boss wasn't always there to walk you through these things, just as you won't always be there. With the proper guidance in the very beginning, your employees will learn how to think for themselves. Encourage them to tap into their strengths in order to find the best solutions for any given problem. Even when they have a new leader in the future, they are going to remember what you first taught them. This is the beginning of your legacy. It is amazing to see how much of a difference you can make, even in the early stages.

Model Lasting Behavior

Your team will learn a lot by watching you work. When you are a leader, it is almost as if you constantly have others shadowing you each day. Remember this as you make your decisions and display your methods. When others see the way you work, they are going to take this as a hint for how they need to work as well. The behavior that you display becomes very important. When you succeed, your employees will know what qualities they need in order to achieve the same results. Alternatively, they are also going to see your mistakes. By being able to witness this behavior, they will know what they need to avoid.

Many leaders wrongfully avoid showing their employees when they make mistakes or when they fail. In an effort to look like they always know what they are doing, a lot of leaders have a problem just being human. Know that every single person is going to mess up at some point in time. This is just the way that life works. What matters most is how you come back from these instances. Own your mistakes; wear them proudly. Have discussions about them with your team and talk about the ways that you can make the situation better or think about what you could have done differently. Let your mistakes become teachable moments.

When you are displaying your strongest skills, make sure you do so in a way that allows your team to see how you got from point A to point B. Being transparent with them will show them that it is also possible for others to succeed. Work with your team and give them step-by-step methods that they can apply to their own lives. A great leader would never have a problem with teaching their team how to achieve the same success. There is a lot of value in patience and humbleness. Understand that it isn't going to come naturally to everyone.

Understand that the behaviors you know and use today all came from other people who once modeled them for you. What made you decide to take on these behaviors? Were you taught them from the beginning or did you pick them up on your own because they appealed to you? Either way, you should always acknowledge the way that you learned them and why they matter to you. This is your way of keeping up other legacies. It all works when the wisdom is being paid forward. Soon enough, your approaches will be used by other people who find value in what you have to share. It is a great feeling, knowing that you can help your team while also helping future teams.

Afterword

As you strive to reach your goals, remember how powerful you already are. You have the ability to speak up for yourself and all of those other women who are fighting the same fight. You do not have to play by the rules that were put into place by those who are already in power. To become a great leader, you must believe in yourself. Own your leadership style and understand that you have great potential. Just because there are barriers that you must face does not mean it isn't possible to prove yourself in the workforce. It takes tenacity and courage to rise above and prove to those around you why you deserve to be there. When you can take the combination of your confidence and your ability to continually win people over, you are going to find many ways to obtain success.

Determine what kind of leader you are and understand that your leadership style can evolve over time. Depending on what is being asked of you at your job, you can transform yourself into exactly what the company needs based on the skills that you already have. As you grow as a leader, you will be able to learn new skills that will keep you current and in the running for the top leadership positions that you desire. When you do not see a clear path for yourself, you will learn how to make one. The women that pave the way, both for themselves and others, are seen as some of the most powerful in the workforce. Don't be afraid to take a risk and create opportunities for yourself.

Allow your skills and determination to get you noticed. It is one thing to be able to list all of your redeeming qualities, but being able to show them with real-life examples will allow you even more growth. Your fears might threaten to get in your way, but when you can convince yourself that you deserve to be there, you will be able to overcome them. Fears are nothing more than doubts that try to pop up when you are facing obstacles. It is understandable that you would have a lot of fears as a woman in a leadership position, but the more that you replace those fears with reaffirming statements about yourself, the easier it will be to overcome them.

Pay attention to those you spend the most time with. These are the people who are going to shape your future. This matters in your professional life as well as your personal life. Since it is thought that the people you are around the most will end up directly influencing you, having awareness about who you are giving your time to is important. Try to seek out those who have the same qualities that you would like to display. Be around people who are powerful, successful, and determined. By keeping this momentum going, you should find it easy to continue to improve on your own skills.

Remember that you do not need to wait for permission to practice your leadership skills. If you are ready to use them, you will find ways in which you can apply them. Stand up for yourself and speak up if you notice any injustices. By getting into this habit, you are going to realize that you are already so powerful with unlimited opportunities to grow. By unlocking your full potential, you are going to make a difference in the workplace and in the world. It is through the efforts of powerful women that the biggest impacts are made. You have a choice to make — let others do the hard work and follow in their footsteps or put in your own work and create results that will inspire others to take action.

Bibliography

5 Tips for Getting Invited to the Executive Leadership Table. (2018, April 3). Retrieved February 18, 2020, from https://tunheim.com/management-consulting-blog/5-tips-for-getting-invited-to-the-executive-leadership-table/

7 Fears You Need to Overcome to Be An Effective Leader - Lolly Daskal | Leadership. (2018, November 13). Retrieved February 19, 2020, from https://www.lollydaskal.com/leadership/7-fears-need-overcome-effective-leader/

17 Reasons Women Make Great Leaders. (2019, January 24). Retrieved February 13, 2020, from https://www.replicon.com/blog/17-reasons-women-make-great-leaders/

Abadi, M. (2019, February 4). Alexandria Ocasio-Cortez's tip to overcome her fear of speaking up in Congress is career advice just about anyone can use. Retrieved February 19, 2020, from https://www.businessinsider.com/alexandria-ocasio-cortez-fear-motivation-2019-2

Andrews, S. (2020). Gender Barriers and Solutions to Leadership. Retrieved February 13, 2020, from https://trainingindustry.com/magazine/issue/gender-barriers-and-solutions-to-leadership/

Checking Your Blind Spot: Ways to find and fix unconscious bias. (n.d.). Retrieved February 21, 2020, from https://www.boyden.com/media/checking-your-blind-spot-ways-to-find-and-fix-unconscious-bias-7627148/index.html

Courtenay-Morris, I. (2018, December 7). Claim Your Seat at the Table: Negotiating Tips for Women | Personal Finance for American Life. Retrieved February 18, 2020, from http://mejopersonalfinance.web.unc.edu/2018/12/claim-your-seat-at-the-table-negotiating-tips-for-women/

Fanning, B. (2020, February 6). 5 Ways the Best Leaders Leave Unforgettable Legacies. Retrieved from https://www.inc.com/ben-fanning/5-ways-the-best-leaders-leave-unforgettable-legacies.html

Female Business Leaders: Global Statistics. (2019, December 12). Retrieved February 13, 2020, from https://www.catalyst.org/research/women-in-management/

Gessen, M. (2018, October 2). Greta Thunberg, the Fifteen-Year-Old Climate Activist Who Is Demanding a New Kind of Politics. Retrieved February 20, 2020, from https://www.newyorker.com/news/our-columnists/the-fifteen-year-old-climate-activist-who-is-demanding-a-new-kind-of-politics

Bibliography

Horton, A. P. (2019, October 18). Women bosses face more discrimination (from both men and women). Retrieved February 13, 2020, from https://www.fastcompany.com/90419052/women-bosses-and-gender-discrimination

Integrating Woman Leaders Foundation. (2015, April 29). 3 Ways to Overcome the Fear of Success. Retrieved February 19, 2020, from http://integrating-womanleaders.com/3-ways-to-overcome-the-fear-of-success/

Kashyap, V. (2019, November 27). 10 Easy Tips to Improve Your Work Performance. Retrieved February 18, 2020, from https://www.proofhub.com/articles/tips-to-improve-work-performance

Mariama-Arthur, K. (2019, March 26). 5 Ways High-Achieving Women Can Break Through the Glass Ceiling. Retrieved February 19, 2020, from https://www.success.com/5-ways-high-achieving-women-can-break-through-the-glass-ceiling/

Mondal, S. (2020, January 5). Diversity And Inclusion: A Beginner's Guide For HR Professionals. Retrieved from https://ideal.com/diversity-and-inclusion/

Moga, B. (2017, May 24). Real Life Examples Of Successful Teamwork [9 Cases] · Activecollab Blog. Retrieved February 20, 2020, from https://activecollab.com/blog/collaboration/real-world-examples-of-successful-teamwork

ProofHub. (2018, March 1). 7 Common Leadership Styles: Which Type of a Leader Are You? Retrieved February 18, 2020, from https://blog.proofhub.com/7-common-leadership-styles-which-type-of-a-leader-are-you-ef23c93bc706

Raines, S. (2020). The Advantages of Knowing Your Leadership Style. Retrieved February 18, 2020, from https://smallbusiness.chron.com/advantages-knowing-leadership-style-18924.html

Riegl, N. T. (2016, January 26). Build Up Your Strength(s) at Work. Retrieved February 18, 2020, from https://www.progressivewomensleadership.com/build-up-your-strengths-at-work/

The FISH! Philosophy Story. (2019, October 23). Retrieved February 20, 2020, from https://www.fishphilosophy.com/fish-philosophy-story/

Toegel, G. (2018, August 16). Where are women leaders today? Retrieved February 13, 2020, from https://www.imd.org/research-knowledge/articles/where-are-women-leaders-today/

Uzzi, B. (2019, February 26). Research: Men and Women Need Different Kinds of Networks to Succeed. Retrieved February 20, 2020, from https://hbr.org/2019/02/research-men-and-women-need-different-kinds-of-networks-to-succeed

Vos, L. J. (2018, February 18). 7 Steps to Personal Brand Building For Women. Retrieved from https://www.ellevatenetwork.com/articles/8741-7-steps-to-personal-brand-building-for-women

Bibliography

When the Boss is a Woman. (2020). Retrieved February 18, 2020, from https://www.apa.org/research/action/boss

Women in Leadership. (2020). Retrieved February 20, 2020, from https://www.scienceofpeople.com/women-in-leadership/

www.ingramcontent.com/pod-product-compliance
Lightning Source LLC
Chambersburg PA
CBHW071019120626
46546CB00003B/1154